Magic Chants for Beginners

Classification, Examples, Structures and Dynamics

Contact: www.HarryEilenstein.de
Harry.Eilenstein@web.de
Harry Eilenstein at youtube

Production and publishing house: BoD – Books on Demand, Norderstedt

ISBN: 9783754303061

Table of Contents

I What is a Chant?

Probably chants, i.e. spell songs are hardly known nowadays – most likely many will have noticed the scene from "Harry Potter and the Half-Blood Prince" where Severus Snape heals Draco Malfoy's injury caused by the spell "Sectrum sempra" by casting a spell that sounded "almost like a chant".

Spell chants, however, have a long tradition. For example, under some texts in the Egyptian Book of the Dead is the reference "well singable spells". Also in the Germanic tradition it is often said that someone sings a spell into his shield and not that he speaks it into his shield.

Spells are therefore apparently sometimes sung and not only spoken. Why? For this, one must first take a closer look at what actually distinguishes chanting from normal speech.

I 1. The Chakras

There are seven main chakras in the life force body, which are its "organs". The "life force circuit" in it is the Kundalini. These organs all have a specific task and dynamics:

The seven main chakras			Symmetry
Name	*Location*	*Function*	
crown chakra	top of the head	spiritual contact	
third eye	between the eyebrows	orientation	
throat chakra	middle of the neck	social self-expression	
heart chakra	chest center	identity	
solar plexus	four finger widths above the navel	physical self-expression	
hara	four fingerbreadths below the navel	inner support	
root chakra	between genitals and anus	physical contact	

These chakras are arranged symmetrically:

- source: inner identity (heart chakra)
- inner pair of chakras: self-expression (solar plexus, throat chakra)
- middle pair of chakras: form (hara, third eye)
- outer pair of chakras: contact (root chakara, crown chakra)

This source and the three pairs have certain properties:

The heart chakra is the source and origin.
This corresponds to the deep sleep consciousness. It is without consciousness content.

The inner pair of chakras (solar plexus, throat chakra) is the uninhibited self-expression, i.e. the vision of what one wants to be and live. In it are all contents of consciousness.
This corresponds to the subconscious mind.

The middle pair of chakras (hara, third eye) concretizes the vision of one's life in contact with the world.
This corresponds to the waking consciousness. In it are the contents of consciousness that are needed in the momentary situation.

The outer pair of chakras (root chakara, crown chakra) is the experience in the here and now.
This corresponds to the state of ecstasy. In it there is only one content of consciousness – this state is one-pointed.

These four areas of the life force body and the psyche can be found in all areas of life.

For example, the body is the source of action (heart chakra).
The unhindered self-expression in doing is dance (inner pair of chakras).
The shaping of the world according to one's own wishes is work (middle pair of chakras).
The one-directed experience of the world is finally enjoying eating and drinking and sex, but also the experience of fear or pain (outer pair of chakras).
=> So, in the doing, from the inside to the outside, the sequence is found: "body – dance – work – sex".

In terms of speech, the source is silence (heart chakra).

The unhindered self-expression is the singing (inner pair of chakras).

The shaping of the world happens with the help of speech (middle pair of chakras).

The one-directed acoustic expression in the here and now is an exclamation, a cry, a groan, crying, laughing, etc. (outer pair of chakras).

=> So, in speaking, from the inside to the outside, the sequence is found: "silence – singing – speaking – exclamation".

Singing thus corresponds to the inner pair of chakras, i.e. the solar plexus and the throat chakra. This direct self-expression, this "letting oneself shine", which is also found in improvised dance and improvised music-making, is the typical element of singing. In singing, what one wants is expressed, one's own vision is made to vibrate.

Singing does not include considerations of where something is possible, with whom or if at all – that belongs to the task of the hara and the third eye, which take care of the concretization of one's own will in the world. The solar plexus and the throat chakra are responsible for unrestrained unfolding of one's own vision – they are only related to one's own identity in the heart chakra.

Now, of course, this does not refer to the specific content of any song that one might sing, but only to the dynamics of singing itself – to the specificity of singing as opposed to speaking.

Singing corresponds to the solar plexus and the throat chakra. This pair of chakras is in turn connected to the subconscious mind. From this it follows that singing must also have a connection to the subconsciousness.

The subconsciousness with all its images is again a part of the collective subconsciousness with its archetypes. The term "archetype" is just another name for "deities".

On the one hand, chanting is suitable for expressing what one wants – because the solar plexus and the throat chakra refer entirely to the heart chakra, in which one's own identity (soul) rests.

On the other hand, chanting is suitable for invoking deities and connecting with them – because chanting has a direct access to the individual subconsciousness and furtheron through this also to the collective subconsciousness.

This results in a division of labor of the four linguistic possibilities in magic:

The roots are in the <u>identity</u>, that is, in the soul in the heart chakra. To find and experience them, <u>silence</u> is the appropriate form.

The awakening of motivation, the shining of the will, the calling of power, the <u>invocation</u> of deities requires a vibration, a clear inner alignment, a freedom from contradiction, a lack of inhibition, a complete self-affirmation. This happens in the solar plexus and in the throat chakra. The appropriate form for this is <u>chanting</u>.

Ordering, structuring, <u>shaping</u>, directing and forming the world is done through the hara and the third eye. The appropriate form for this is <u>speech</u>.

The <u>grounding</u>, the "bringing to the point", "one's own signature" at the end of the ritual (the Indian "Ho!", the Christian "Amen"), the sending into the world of the magical effect happens in the root chakra and in the crown chakra through a single sound or through a single word. The appropriate form for this is the <u>exclamation</u>.

Consequently, the magic chant has many functions:

- to make one's inner self vibrate as a unity,
- to bring oneself into a unity of alignment,
- to vibrate in self-affirmation and self-love,
- to fill one's consciousness with what one really is,
- to express oneself,
- to let one's own will shine
- to bring oneself into harmony with other magicians in the ritual,
- to connect one's own individual subconsciousness (images) with the collective subconsciousness (archetypes),
- to summon power,
- to connect with a deity,
  etc.

Telepathy and telekinesis also belong to the sphere of individual subconsciousness and collective subconsciousness – they are the ability of perception and action of the individual and collective subconsciousness. Since ultimately all magic can be traced back to telepathy and telekinesis, chanting is a way to activate this magical ability to perceive and this magical ability to act.

The individual subconsciousness and collective subconsciousness are also the areas of the life force – thus singing connects also to the life force.

By magical chanting, one can enter a dream-journey-like state in which one is connected to the inner imagery – not only to the imagery in one's own subconscious, but also to the imagery in others and in the collective subconsciousness in general. Both dream journey and chanting are a connection and coordination of waking consciousness and subconsciousness including the collective subconsciousness.

The chant is the "current connection" of the ritual, the construction of which is done by language. The functioning of the "ritual machine" then leads to the exclamation. The whole thing is created out of silence.

By chanting, one awakens the vision of oneself in oneself and also the deities who then come to the chanting person.

I 2.   The Transitions between Singing and Speech

The transition from speech to singing has several aspects, as singing also has several characteristics.

I 2. a)   The Vibration

The basic element of singing is vibration. This can best be seen by speaking the word "one" once and singing it once. Singing contains a constant power – just as self-expression is a constant radiation of one's own individuality.

A spoken word is like a handicraft work – something is brought into a fitting form. The sung word, on the other hand, is like a swinging – something receives power and is held powerfully.

I 2. b)   The Melody of Speech

There is not simply "singing" and "speech", but many transitions between these two acoustic means of expression.

At the very "speech end" of this scale is toneless speech, i.e. speech without speech melody – which sounds like an ancient computer.

The strange technical sound of such a toneless speech already shows that speech is rarely completely "without music". Someone who speaks completely without any accentuation is probably completely resigned – his hara is cut off from his solar plexus and his third eye from his throat chakra. As a result, the person can no longer let his feelings and motivation (inner pair of chakras) flow into his relation to the world (middle pair of chakras).

A person who tries to assert himself with great emphasis, on the other hand, will give melody to his speech with a loud voice, with strong emphasis, with pauses and many other rhetorical means.

The simplest form of chanting is the singing of all words in the same pitch and tone length as can be found, for example, in Tibetan temple chants, in which only the last note of a text is sung slightly lower.

Quite similar is the Gregorian chant, which is also still quite simple, but varies in pitch and more rarely in pitch length. With Gregorian chant, too, the pitch usually drops a little at the end.

Likewise, the "intoning" of god names and the chanting of runes usually occurs without meter or rhythm on a pitch that remains constant from beginning to end.

Finally, there is a proper melody in the song.

I 2. c) The Beat

The beat is not a necessary element of a song – for example, the Gregorianic gets along without a beat, and in many Indian and ancient Amerindian songs the beat changes very frequently. In today's music, music without a beat is found only very rarely – an example is e.g. the first piece "Cluster one" on the CD "The Division Bell" by Pink Floyd.

The beat is the division of note length in a way by which the note clusters form units that are always the same length – so in a 4/4 time signature after four quarter notes, the new beat always begins with a new note. This leads to the fact that one can clap along with the beat.

The beat has the effect of repeating a melodic element, which in turn has the effect of giving the melody a predictable element that gives it power and consistency. The beat has the effect of causing the singing to vibrate, thereby supporting the vibration that comes originates from singing. The beat builds up an "avalanche of power," so to speak, which is confirmed by each measure and thus becomes greater.

Thus, a spell chant with a beat will generally have more power than a spell chant without a beat.

The different measures have a different character. The simplest and most common measure is the 4/4 time signature. It is also the measure that gives the most power to the chant.

The 3/4 time signature has something swinging about it and conveys lightness rather than power, which is why it is often found in couple dancing (waltzes, for example).

The 5/4 time is difficult to grasp as a rhythm because it is usually an alternation between a 3/4 time and a 2/4 time measure – i.e., not a steady continuous beat. The 5/4 time therefore requires great alertness.

In oriental music there are often much more complex measures like the sequence "3/4 – 3/4 – 3/4 – 4/4". These complex measures, which are also used in dance, require a high level of concentration from the musicians, singers and dancers and therefore promote the presence of the singers in this chant.

These complex measures are more suited for promoting one-pointedness and the state of "be here now" than for calling power and evoking a dream-journey-like state.

Almost all spell songs have a 4/4 time signature.

I 2. d)   The Rhythm

The rhythm is an emphasis within a measure. This can be done by playing the first note of each measure louder, for example, or by a drum beat on that note, and also by a particular arrangement of notes in each measure such as two eighth notes at the beginning of each measure.

While the beat gives power to the chant, the rhythm gives color to the chant. Rhythm can be restrained, driving, floating, and many other things. You can often recognize a musical style by its rhythm – for example, in reggae, the 2nd and 4th quarter notes are always emphasized in 4/4 time.

The rhythm should fit the content of the magic song and should be rather simple – e.g. have an emphasis on the first note in each measure.

I 2. e)   The Scale

There is singing that does not need a scale – you just sing as you go. This kind of singing can sometimes be heard in small children, about 2-4 years old, when they are singing to tell themselves something.

As a rule, however, there is a scale, i.e. fixed pitches that may occur in a song.

The simplest scale consists of the tones that can easily be perceived as harmonious to a fundamental. For example, the octave has a frequency twice as high as the fundamental – it is twice as "bright/high" as the fundamental. The fifth has a frequency 3/2 times as high as the fundamental; the fourth has a frequency 4/3 times as high as the fundamental, etc.

From the five simplest of these pitch ratios, which can therefore also be heard and sung in the simplest way, the pentatonic ("five-tone") results. It is quite certainly the oldest form of the scale, which can also be found in the spontaneous singing of children.

By the addition of two further tones one arrives at the scale which is usual among other things in the western culture and which consists of seven tones.

By adding another five tones ("half tones"), we get the scale of twelve tones with equal pitch intervals, which can be found, for example, on the piano as the white keys (scale of seven tones) and the black keys (the five added tones). These additional notes add more "color" to the sound, which is why this scale is also called "chromatic" ("colorful").

Even more complex are the oriental scales, which add another six notes, each of which is halfway between two successive notes of the chromatic scale. While the pitch spacing in the chromatic scale is the same everywhere, the spacing in the oriental "intermediate" quarter tones is only half as large – thus allowing for much finer nuances.

Finally, in the Indian ragas, for example, there is the peculiarity that when one changes from a high note to a low note (from right to left on the piano), one uses a different scale than when one changes from a low note to a high note (from left to right on the piano).

These complex scales, like the complex measures, have the effect of making the singer awake, focused, and present, but preventing him from entering a dream-journey-like state. Therefore, most spell songs are pentatonic, that is, they use the simplest of scales.

I 2. f) The Words

First of all, the words of the song should represent as accurately as possible the intended effect of the magic song.

However, there is a great variety in the magic songs in terms of the words as well.

There is a form of magic song that does not require any words at all and that has become quite popular for some time, especially in spiritual-therapeutic contexts. In it, everyone simply sings an "a" or another vowel together at any pitch and length, both of which can be varied constantly by all participants.

This technique creates a shared space in which everyone, as they are, is present and part of the whole. Therefore, this improvised singing technique is well suited for creating a bond among the participants and for increasing the energy potential in the community.

However, one can also use this wordless chanting alone – e.g. in a temple, a church, in front of a statue of a god, facing the full moon, etc., to establish a contact with the deity, the moon, etc..

In doing so, the inner desire, the longing, the intention then flows right into the chant without taking on a specific form by words. This can be very beneficial – and it gives the mind a break …

A variant of this wordless singing is improvised singing. For example, you can sit

13

down and sing a wish to the improvised playing on the guitar – with the words and the melody that arises just out of the moment. It is not at all a matter of artistic quality and perfection, but only of singing what one wants at the moment.

This method, if applied from the heart, i.e. without inner contradictions, is extremely effective from a magical point of view.

The simplest, fixed song texts consist of only one word – they are chanted mantras. However, this form is very rare.

The next level are the chanted mantras, which consist of a short phrase. They are quite common and popular.

The next level is the short songs ("chants"), which consist of a short verse repeated over a long period of time. This form is also very common.

A variant of this type of chant is the multi-strophic song, which, however, again requires increased concentration and is therefore not so well suited for achieving a dream-journey-like state.

This is especially true of the songs with stanzas, which consist of two alternating lyrics that differ only slightly because you have to stay very awake to know which variation you are on.

Finally, there is the song with many verses, which one either sings only once or repeats only a few times. These songs are not very good for creating a trance state. They probably have such an effect only if they are sung daily, for example.

The song should be from a suitable tradition if you want to sing it in a certain context that is influenced by a certain tradition. However, there are also many contexts in which songs from different traditions can be used together.

The text should have a fixed meter, i.e. a regular alternation of stressed and unstressed syllables – this is the "speech beat", so to speak.

The text should also contain rhyme – this is also a form of "speech meter." There are many forms of rhyme: end rhyme, staff rhyme (same initial letters), half-rhyme (same vowel plus following consonant inside the word), clustering of the same vowel in one line, content rhyme (repetition of a verse with the same statement, same grammatical structure, but with different words) etc. There is a very great variety in rhymes.

I 2. g) Repetition

Repetition is an important element to build up tension, to invoke power, and to get into a dream-travel-like state ("trance").
These possible repetitions are:

- same pitches (fixed scale)
- beat
- rhythm
- repetition of the whole text
- meter
- rhymes in the text
- refrain
- repetition of the melody
- singing on every day, on certain festivals or the like
- singing in several generations (traditional songs)

I 2. h) The Sound

The essential element of singing is the vibration. Simple singing is possible for just about anyone – even if one may be a bit short of breath or one's voice may sometimes croak a bit.

However, one can achieve a whole different sonority by practice and specific training of one's own voice (which should be, above all, a freeing of the voice from blockages).
This greater sonority has five important aspects:

1. The most well-known element is certainly the duration in which one can sing a note. This "vocal endurance" improves by frequent singing, by sports, by breathing exercises, but also by methods through which one gets to know one's breath better.

2. Natural vibrato is a vibration of the voice with the frequency of about 6Hz. This is the frequency at which also the subconsciousness vibrates, as can be determined, for example, by measuring brain waves during dreaming with the help of an EEG. Laughter, crying, trembling, the orgasm reflex etc. also have this frequency.

It is an extremely pleasant feeling when one's own voice vibrates at this frequency when singing!

You can also hear this vibrato in many singers if you pay attention to it once. However, it is often not the natural vibrato of the voice that appears when one "simply lets one's own voice do its thing", but an embellishment of the singing that is deliberately used.

3. The third element is the overtones of the voice. They are created when the air resonates not only in the throat, but also in the lungs, the mouth, the sinuses, etc.. This makes the voice sound fuller, "richer" and "more colorful".

4. From these three elements a larger volume of one's own voice results almost by itself, which is effortless and also does not seem obtrusive. A deliberately greater volume usually sounds strained, slightly pressed, hoarse, etc., i.e. not at all pleasant.

5. The fifth element is the creation of a standing wave. This means, on the one hand, that you yourself as a whole begin to vibrate in the tone you are singing, and on the other hand, that you can use the space you are in as a soundbox for your own voice. If one can create a standing wave with one's own voice, the entire room resonates with it, which once again leads to a significant increase in the power, fullness, sound and also the effortlessness of singing.

Probably, to learn the last four of these five aspects of singing, one will need personal instruction. However, you can also develop your voice significantly simply by singing often.

A good method to develop your voice is the so-called "Lichtenberger Method". It consists on the one hand of physical exercises and on the other hand of methods that dissolve the psychological blockages of the voice.

One element of this method works as follows: Sing an "a". Listen to this "a": Are you short of breath? Is your voice quite low? Is your voice hoarse or breathy? Allow your voice to sing this quality – the shortness of breath, the lowness of your voice and so on. This is a bid easier if you talk to your voice: "Hello voice – please give my shortness of breath voice." The just sing and listen … If feelings arise during this singing then you may lend your voice to this feelings. This may soon become a journey of discovery full of unexpected sounds and feelings. This method is very effective.

However, there are also many other schools – for example, in some training courses in classical singing Kundalini yoga is used. In this approach, the power of Kundalini, i.e. the life force flowing in the body, is connected directly with the voice. This is a very direct approach to give the singing a magical effect. The central image here is that you have a burning lake of oil in your abdomen, the fire of which flames upward and outward through your throat when you are singing.

There are also classical methods of voice training, but they are not particularly differentiated-empathetic: For example, the Roman politician and orator Cicero stood by the sea and practiced speaking loudly with a pebble under his tongue, so that he would then have a loud, powerful (and therefore convincing) voice under the much more favorable circumstances in the assembly hall and without a pebble under his tongue.

A full, melodious voice is not absolutely necessary to successfully singing magic chants with a great magical effect. However, the healing and training of one's own voice is closely related to self-healing and is already from this point of view very conducive to effective magic – both in singing and in magic, the identity in the heart chakra should be able to flow outward through the three pairs of chakras as undisturbed as possible.

I 2. i) The Community

Magical chanting is in many cases done by individuals, but especially in a traditional setting there is also much communal chanting.

The simplest possible form is the collective chanting of a mantra, chant or song ("chorus").

This chanting becomes somewhat more complex when it is polyphonic. However, this directs the chanting in the direction of awake concentration and not in the direction of magical trance.

Another form of communal chanting is the precentor, who sings one or a few verses, which are then repeated by all together. The disadvantage of this form, from a magical point of view, is that there is no steady flow of the chant.

The situation is similar with the alternating individual singing of different texts and the joint singing of a chorus.

On the other hand, there is somewhat more power in the alternating singing, in which individual singers and the choir alternately sing short verses, they refer to each other and sometimes form a kind of conversation. In this way, the singing as a whole forms a clearer unity.

A special form of choral singing, if one wants to call it that, is the joint recitation of a spoken text.

I 2. j) Summary

According to these considerations, the most effective and therefore ideal chant would be as follows:

- The song has appropriate lyrics.
- The text is short: a mantra verse or a chant (short verse).
- The text has a fixed meter.
- The lyrics have rhymes.
- The song has a 4/4 time signature.
- The rhythm of the song fits its content and purpose.
- The melody has a pentatonic scale – possibly also a seven-tone scale.
- The song is sung frequently: every day, every time on a particular occasion (healing, feast, etc.), over several generations, etc.
- The singer(s) have in their voice endurance, the natural vibrato as well as rich overtones, which allows them to reach an effortless volume and create a standing wave in the place where they are.
- Singing in a community gives more power to the singing, but it also restricts the singing to the commen intention of the subjects of the community.

II   New Creations

In many cases, traditional songs can be found that are suitable for a particular purpose as spell songs.

Probably the largest collection of songs from around the world can be viewed at http://www.recmusic.org/lieder/. About 50,000 songs are listed there. However, it is quite difficult to find something there – you need a very clear idea of what you are looking for, and a lot of patience to boot.

Sometimes, however, you may not be successful in finding a suitable song. Then there are again different possibilities.

II 1.   Already Existing Lyrics

Sometimes you find a poem or a "song without melody" whose lyrics express what you are striving for.

For example, if you want to have more romance and nature in your life, and you like the hobbit's wandering song from Tolkien's "Lord of the Rings", you can use this song as a magic song – even if it was not actually written as a magic song.

II 2.   Songs without a Specific Tradition

In some cases, there is also a magical-spiritual song by a composer that is well suited for one's own purposes. For example, the song "fire prayer" by Denean can be used as a fire invocation.

When searching for such songs, you will quickly find that there are quite a few songs on some subjects, but almost none on others.

II 3.   Use of a Non-Spiritual Song

It also happens that one discovers a song or a song text that actually does not come from any spiritual context, but is nevertheless extremely well suited as an invocation, such as the song "A Elbereth Gilthoniel" from Tolkien's "Lord of the Rings".

19

II 4. The "Spirit Language"

A special form of song lyrics is the "spirit language". This term is used by the North American Indians to refer to lyrics that consist of only a few known words and many a "hey" and "ho", and like syllables. These songs are usually found on dream journeys, vision quests, and so on.

Sometimes such songs appear spontaneously. For example, I was once at a Rainbow Camp, where we danced and drummed around a fire in the evening. There my she-wolf (my power animal) began to sing in me in the "spirit language". At first I sang it only inwardly, then quietly to myself, but finally I sang it aloud with all my might. To my great amazement, everyone finally sang along. I have rarely felt the power of my she-wolf so clearly within me and especially around me.

More frequent than the "spontaneous singing in the spirit language" is the "speaking in tongues", i.e. speaking languages that one has never learned ("glossolalia").

Within a fixed tradition, songs found by someone on a vision quest sometimes become traditional songs used for several generations.

II 5. The Search for a New Song

If you need a song on a particular subject, but can't find one anywhere, you have to write it yourself. This may take a while. You need a suitable text and a suitable melody for it – and both are not necessarily immediately at hand.

When I started to lead sweat lodges, I was missing a song for the Great Spirit (Manitou, Wakan Tanka), which is also called "Great Mystery", i.e. for the source of life in all things (Chinese: Tao).

First I tried it with German sentences, then with English verses, but nothing of it convinced me. Thereupon I simply sang to myself for a few days – mostly the Dakota name of the "Great Secret", i.e. "Wakan tanka" appeared in this song. Even my attempts to compose a verse out of "Wakan tanka" and some spirit language syllables felt wrong.

But finally, all of a sudden a verse with melody appeared in me that convinced me – it felt right and powerful. I wrote it down and sang it to myself for the next few days, "Wakan tanka hey-o-ah."

However, I thought it was actually much too short, so I searched for more verses. But finally I realized that any kind of extension felt wrong and was a weakening, so I stuck with that one short verse.

I then used this spirit language song in the sweat lodge for calling wakan tanka and found that it worked well for that and had the effect I wanted.

It has become apparent over time that the easiest way to find a song is to use four steps:

1. Immerse yourself in the theme of the song until you can feel its quality within you.

2. Look for a melody that has a sound that fits the theme.

3. Insert the essential statements about the theme into this melody.

4. sing the song and see if it flows freely and feels as desired.

III   One's Own Song

There is a special group of songs – the songs that refer to oneself: to one's own soul, to one's own power animal, one's own power plant, one's own power stone, one's own patron deity, and so on.

For these beings one can sometimes find already existing suitable songs – most easily usually for one's own power animal and one's own patron deity. In many cases, however, one must become creative oneself, if one would like to have a suitable song, e.g. for one's own power stone – for which there are almost no songs at all.

III 1.   Silence

On the level of the heart chakra (deep sleep consciousness) it is very easy to find the appropriate song: It is quite simply silence, that is, meditation, in which one lets go of all thoughts, feelings and images and is only consciousness, that is aware of itself but contains nothing. This is, even if it may sound a little absurd, a very fulfilling state.

III 2.   One's Own Song

One can experience one's own soul and its allies (power animal, power plant, power stone) as well as its origin (patron deity) on the level of the solar plexus and the throat chakra (subconscious) by a dream journey to one's own center. This may then become the basis for writing songs to these beings, these allies of oneself, these aspects of oneself.

III 3.   The Hymn to Oneself

On the level of the hara and the third eye (waking consciousness) one can write a "hymn to oneself", in which one expresses, arranges, summarizes and puts into the most suitable form what one knows about oneself.

For this, the dream journeys to one's own center, one's own biography, one's own horoscope, one's dream diary etc. are important aids.

One can simply begin to collect simple "I am ..." sentences about oneself. You can also try it with "I do ..." sentences. The only criterion for these sentences is that you can say that they are really true.

If you can't think of anything at first, you can try with very simple things like:

> I am a woman.
> I am an Aquarius.
> I am a mother.

Probably you will soon become more creative and come up with more "colorful" phrases like:

> I am a dancer.
> I love the sunrise.
> I am a passionate lover.

Now, if you add spiritual experiences and the like, the whole thing becomes more and more contoured:

> I sit there in silence like Buddha.
> My power animal is a panther.
> My power plant is the date palm.
> My power stone is the smoke obsidian.
> I know astral projection.

When you get the first dozen sentences together, you will probably enjoy it and the next sentences will flow much more easily from the pen.

Then, when you have found two or three dozen such sentences, you can begin to arrange them in such a way that they have an order that is pleasant to read, and the whole gradually acquires the character of a hymn to yourself.

You can add to this hymn every time you find a new "true sentence" about yourself and possibly restructure it.

It is worthwhile to read this hymn aloud once. It is even more effective if a good friend is listening.

This hymn can then also be a basis for the text for a song, e.g. to your own soul. For this, the appropriate verses from this hymn must be selected and possibly recomposed, reshaped, put into a verse measure, provided with a rhyme, etc. Then, when the text is ready, one can look for a melody for it.

III 4. The Presence

At the level of the root chakra and the crown chakra (ecstatic state), it is a matter of being one with what one is, or with what one wants at the moment. In this, the words are usually reduced to a single word or exclamation such as "Yes!" This "Yes!" can refer, for example, to the hymn to oneself or to one's own song.

You may also end your song with a "Yes!" or a "Ho!" or the like. There are some amerindian songs that incorporate several "Ho!"-calls into the song – this is quite powerful.

III 5. The Four Ways

The source is the experience of one's own soul in silence. Possibly one then takes dream journeys and gets to know the variety of what one's own soul wants to express itself as. This can then be summarized by a "hymn to oneself". Through a further summary and a setting to music, this then becomes a song to one's own soul or several songs to the soul, to the power animal, to the patron deity, etc.

This hymn and these songs can be a help to remember again and again what one actually really is and to align oneself with it again, so that one can then exclaim "Yes!" with conviction and do exactly what one wants to do at the moment.

These four ways are:

> the silence,
> one's own song,
> the hymn to oneself and
> the exclamation in the presence in the moment.

IV   The Use of Spell Songs

There are many different traditions and possible uses for magic songs in magic, cult and religion.

IV 1.   The Application

In Western magic, contemporary spell chanting is largely limited to intoning the names of gods and the like in rituals.

Free, wordless chanting occurs primarily in group therapy, firewalking, Wicca (witchcraft cult), and the like.

Communally sung songs are mainly found in the major religions such as Christianity. These include antiphonal singing, choruses, and the like.

The mantras and the chants have been adopted primarily from India, but to some extent also from the North American Indians. However, they are mainly used in the Indian-oriented cult and in sweat lodge ceremonies.

However, this has not always been the case. As the remnants of spiritual songs in the written tradition show, Indo-European culture must once have possessed a rich spiritual song heritage. Sometimes there are references by missionaries to "shameful" songs in the cult of the pagans, and in some cases the texts of some songs have survived.

The keepers of the tradition are consistently called "singers" and not "orators" with the Indo-Europeans (Greeks: rapsodes; Germans: skalds; Celts: bards, etc.). From this it follows that the tradition preserved by them consisted mainly of songs.

There are almost no melodies handed down. At first, the "pagan songs" were mentioned (if at all) only in passing and disapprovingly by the missionaries; then, occasionally, their texts were recorded by scholars; but by the time musical notation was sufficiently developed and known, most of the melodies had already fallen into oblivion.

Only in the traditions that remained alive until modern times are melodies of magic songs known.

IV 2.   Personal Preferences

As with all things, everyone must look at what suits him and what is effective for him in the case of magic songs. Perhaps one finds acceptable only the intonation of God's names and the like, perhaps one would prefer to cast spells only by singing …

Communal chanting usually requires a minimum level of agreement on a particular cult – such as participation in a sweat lodge ceremony.

IV 3.   Effectiveness

A method that makes you uncomfortable is usually not going to work very well. The same is true of a tradition that one dislikes.

The essential thing is always a clear, unopposed motivation. Chanting helps to make this motivation shine, to reach the state of connectedness with the individual subconsciousness and the collective subconsciousness ("trance"), and thereby to give power to the ritual. For this, chanting is not absolutely necessary, but it is a good tool.

V Magic Songs

The following songs are only a very small selection. Especially the Indian, African and Native American traditions are very rich in spell songs.

Some of these songs can be found under the song title on youtube, for example, so that you can listen to the melody and do not have to read and sing it from the notes.

The songs listed here have a rather general character, in order to be usable for as many people as possible, but of course one can also compose and use songs for passing an exam, for healing from a certain disease, for obtaining a building plot, etc.

V 1.   The Great Mystery

V 1. a)   Wakan tanka

Lyrics and melody: Harry Eilenstein

The term "Wakan tanka" of the Dakota Indians means "Great Mystery." It means life, the gods, the world and the fact that anything exists at all.

This song is sung a bid speedy and urgent.

Hey Wakan tanka, hey-o-ah!

V 1. b)   Ho'zhong song

Lyrics and melody: traditional, Navaho (Arizona).

"Ho'zhong" originates from the Navaho language and means "rightness."
 Rightness is the central concept in all mythological worldviews. It includes the meanings of "rightness," "rhythm," "beauty," "efficacy," and, in later times, "justice.
 This rightness is the main characteristic of the "Great Mystery".
 The individual share of a person in this correctness is his soul.

The "x" notes at the end of lines 7, 8, and 9 ("Ho!") are not sung, but spoken or shouted.

The quality of beauty, rightness, and truth is called Ho'zhong, Hozhoni, or Hozhonji by the Navahos.

It is helpful, when singing this song, to imagine first enveloping oneself in beauty (lines 1-5) and then also allowing it to radiate outward from within (lines 7-9), for ultimately these songs are intended primarily as aids to the inner imaginings that are what ultimately bring about inner and thus outer change.

In Tibet, it is said that the life force follows the imagination – which is why positive thinking is also useful and why, for example, a hunting spell works, in which one represents a successful hunt.

In China this connection is very vividly represented by the dragon (life force) chasing the wish ball (imagination).

V 2.   The Goddess

V 2. a)   Goddesses

Text and melody: anonymous, from Feminist Wicca

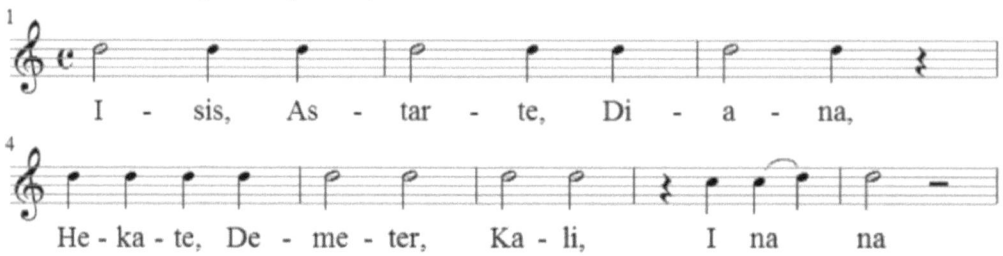

I - sis,   As - tar - te,   Di - a - na,
He - ka - te, De - me - ter,   Ka - li,   I na na

These seven goddesses are different figures of the Mother Goddess from Egypt, Mesopotamia and from the Indo-Europeans.

The names Isis and Astarte go back to the Neolithic mother goddess on her throne, next to which sat a panther on each side. Both names go back to Aset, which means "seat, throne."

Diana is a feminine form of the Indo-European name "Dhyaus", which means "sun". It is an epithet of the sky goddess who gives birth to the sun in the morning.

The meaning of the name of the Greek goddess Hekate is unclear. She was originally the mother of rebirth in the afterlife. Later her meaning narrowed down first to the way to the otherworld and finally to the gate to the otherworld.

Demeter means "barley mother." Through the parable between the destiny of humans and that of grain, the goddess of rebirth also became the mother of grain.

Inanna is a common development in Mesopotamia of the word mama for mother. The first letter „I" is an invocation-call like „Oh!" in „Oh God!"

V 2. b)   Goddesses

Text and melody: anonymous, from the Wiccan tradition

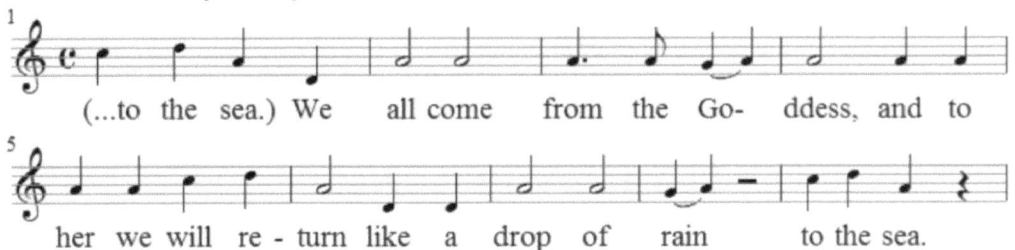

(...to the sea.) We all come from the Go-ddess, and to
her we will re - turn like a drop of rain to the sea.

The song "We all come from the Goddess" has a special dynamic in that there is no pause between the end of one repetition of this chant (" … to the sea.") and the beginning of the next repetition ("We …"). As a result, one is inclined to keep singing the chant on and on.

V 2. c)   Goddesses

Lyrics and melody: Harry Eilenstein

We call to Fre- ya, we call to Frigg, we call to Nan- na, to Jörd,
We dance for Si- gyn, we pray to Sif, we sing for I- dun all day

We call to Freya, we call to Frigg,
We call to Nanna, we call to Jörd,
We dance for Sigyn, we pray to Sif,
We sing for Idun all Day.

Freya: northern Germanic mother goddess, goddess of love and rebirth.
Frigg: southern Germanic mother goddess, goddess of love and rebirth

31

Nanna: mother goddess and goddess of rebirth
Jörd: earth goddess
Sigyn: goddess of the afterlife
Sif: earth goddess and grain goddess
Idun: goddess of the apples of eternal youth

V 2. d) Earth Goddess

Text and melody: anonymous, from the Rainbow tradition (possibly Amerindian)

This is probably, next to the sun dance song "Kuaté", the best known of the songs sung in Germany in the sweat lodges. That it has an Indian origin, as is stated from time to time, is at least quite uncertain – in any case it has become known by the Rainbow mid-summer festivals.

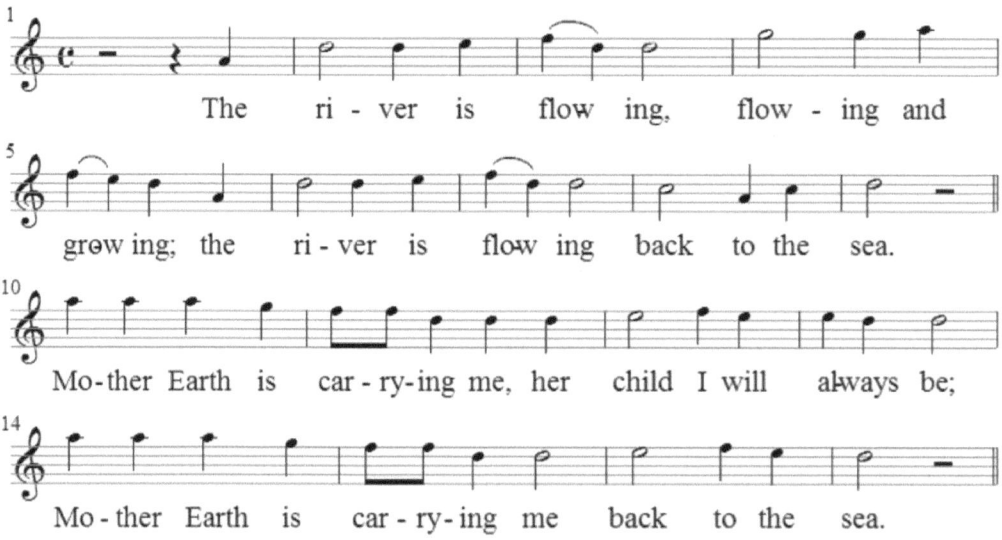

The ri - ver is flow ing, flow - ing and grow ing; the ri - ver is flow ing back to the sea.

Mo-ther Earth is car - ry-ing me, her child I will always be; Mo - ther Earth is car - ry- ing me back to the sea.

V 2. e) Earth Goddess

Text and melody: anonymous (possibly Amerindian)

This is one of the songs frequently sung in European sweat lodges and also in other ceremonies. Its origin is possibly Amerindian, but nothing can be found out for sure about its roots.

V 2. f) Earth Goddess

Text and melody: anonymous (probably Amerindian)

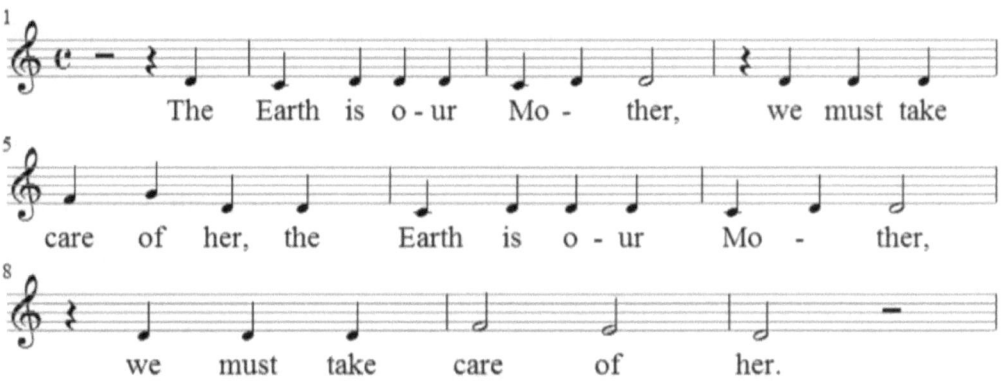

The following three stanzas may be sung to the same melody:

(stanza 2) *Its sacred ground we walk upon with every step we take*
Its sacred ground we walk upon with every step we take

(stanza 3) *The Earth is my mother I must take care of her*
The Earth is my mother I must take care of her

(stanza 4) *Its sacred ground I walk upon with every step I take*
Its sacred ground I walk upon with every step I take

The difference between stanzas 1/2 and 3/4 is only that in 1/2 the community sings "we", and in 3/4 each individual sings "I", making it clearer that really each individual is meant.

Each time one of these stanzas has been repeated several times and one changes to the following stanza, the following verses are sung:

(Intermediate stanza) *Unite, my people, be as one!*
Unite, my people, be as one!

The whole thing is an alternating chant: stanzas 1-4 are sung by the Amerindians or the people in the sweat lodge, while the intermediate stanza is sung by Mother Earth and is addressed to the people. This voice is actually sung by a precentor or the sweat lodge leader (or someone else) alone. If a community is skilled in sweat lodge and wants to try more complex forms than "everyone sings everything," then they can also sing this in the ritual as an antiphonal chant.

The song is a conversation between humans and Mother Earth, structured as follows:

Humans (us): stanza 1 (repeat several times).
   Mother Earth: Intermediate stanza
Humans (us): stanza 2 (repeat several times)
   Mother Earth: Intermediate stanza
Humans (me): stanza 3 (repeat several times)
   Mother Earth: Intermediate stanza
Humans (me): stanza 4 (repeat several times)
   Mother Earth: Intermediate stanza

Humans (us): stanza 1 (repeat several times)
Mother Earth: Intermediate stanza
Humans (us): stanza 2 (repeat several times)

V 2. g)   Moon Goddess

Text and melody: anonymous (Amerindian inspired)

The melody of this song corresponds to that of the song "The river is flowing".

V 2. h)   Moon Goddess

Lyrics and melody: traditional, Seneca (New York, Oklahoma, Southern Canada)

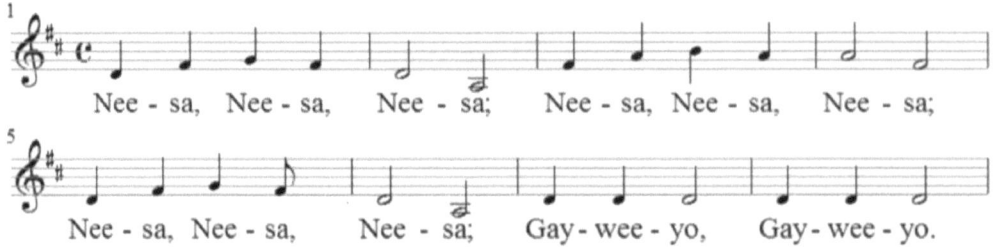

Nee - sa, Nee - sa, Nee - sa; Nee - sa, Nee - sa, Nee - sa;

Nee - sa, Nee - sa, Nee - sa; Gay - wee - yo, Gay - wee - yo.

"Neesa" means "grandmother moon" and "Gayweeyo" means "creator/creation."
The Seneca are the westernmost of the five Iroquois peoples who formed a large community. They lived in southwestern Lake Ontario and settled in New York State, Oklahoma, and mid-southern Canada, among other places. The Seneca called themselves Onodowohgah, meaning "the people of the ridge." They lived by farming and fishing.

V 2. i)   Corn Goddess

Text and melody: traditional, Pawnee (Nebraska, Kansas, South Dakota)

"Atira" is the Pawnee name for the corn mother. This goddess was worshipped by all corn-growing Indians in the Americas – among the Incas, for example, she was called "Sara-Mama." Her Greek equivalents would be Demeter or her daughter Kore/ Persephone.
"Nawa" in the Pawnee language means to summon something ("Hither!"), to greet something, and to be grateful for coming ("thanks") – "Nawa" is, so to speak, an invitation filled with thanks, i.e. the wish, filled with trust and gratitude, for the goddess to come to the people.
This attitude can be found e.g. also with Christ, who thankes God before his miracles (and not only afterwards) that God will perform the miracle immediately on Christ's request. Very clearly this is described e.g. with the raising of Lazarus from death.

Today this attitude would probably be called an extreme form of "positive thinking" – which according to Christ can move mountains …

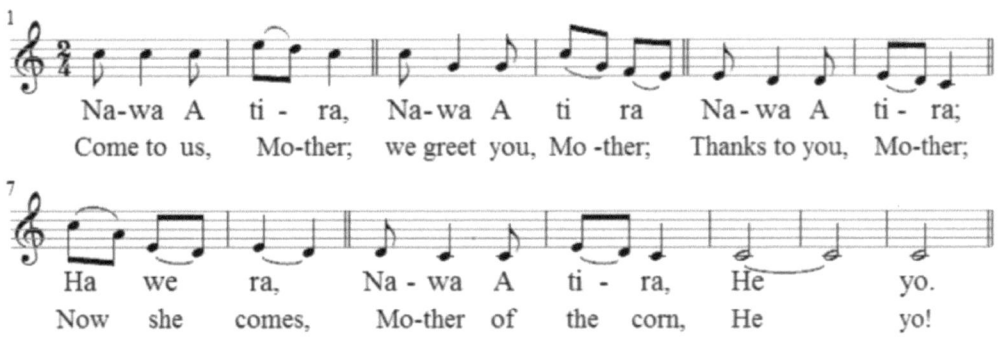

Na-wa A ti - ra, Na-wa A ti ra Na-wa A ti - ra;
Come to us, Mo-ther; we greet you, Mo -ther; Thanks to you, Mo-ther;

Ha we ra, Na - wa A ti - ra, He yo.
Now she comes, Mo-ther of the corn, He yo!

V 2. j) Durgha

Text and melody: traditional, India

Durgha is the most revered goddess in India. She is, among other things, the elemental force, the life force, often called "Shakti". Her name means "the hard to reach one", which could indicate her as the goddess of afterlife and rebirth (afterlife = the hard to reach place).

Hey Ma . Dur- gha, hey Ma . Dur- gha, hey Ma . Dur- . gha, Jay Jay . Ma.

V 2. k) Isis

Text and melody: Harry Eilenstein

This Isis chant is written in ancient Egyptian.

Isis, Isis, netjeret werer, ich di ankh en-i!
Ma'at, hotep, heka, reshut en hehe!
Isis, Isis, netjeret nefer, ich di hai en-i!
Ma'at, hotep, heka, reshut en hehe!

Isis, Isis, great goddess – give me life!
Beauty, peace, magic, joy forever!
Isis, Isis, good goddess – give me joy!
Beauty, peace, magic, joy forever!

Ma'at is rightness, the right measure, beauty, harmony and organic cohesion. From this originates Hotep (peace of mind) and Heka (magic). These in turn lead to Reshut (joy). This sequence can be seen as the foundation of the ancient Egyptian worldview.

V 3.   The Gods

V 3. a)   Aesir

Text: traditional, Germanic (Scandinavia, Iceland)
Melody: Harry Eilenstein

There are no melodies from the Germanic tribes, but plenty of spells have been handed down, so that one can fall back on old texts when writing spell songs.

In the Sigdrifa song the Valkyrie Sigdrifa speaks the following verses to her beloved Sigurd/Siegfried:

"Hail to you day and hail to you day-sons,
Hail night and nourishing earth:
With wrathless eyes look upon us
And give us sitting-ones victory.

Hail to you Aesir, hail to you Aesynja,
Hail to thee, fertile field!
Word and wisdom grant us noble two
And ever healing hands!"

The "day" is the sun god Dag (Tyr); his sons are the gods.

The night and earth goddess is also the otherworld goddess who gives birth to the former sun-god-godfather Tyr again in the morning.

"Unwrathful" means "mild, kind, benevolent."

Aesynja = female Aesir

This text sounds with lines of equal length and verse meter in both stanzas and translated into German as follows (the stressed syllables are underlined):

Heil Dir Tag und Heil euch Tages-Söhnen,
Heil Dir Nacht und nähr'nde Erde:
Schaut auf uns mit milden Augen
Und gebt uns Sitzenden den Sieg.

Heil euch Asen, Heil euch Asen-Frauen,
Heil Euch, Früchte-reicher Boden!
Wort und Weisheit gebt uns beiden,

Und heil'nde Hände allezeit!

An english version would be:

Hail, oh day and hail, oh sons of daytime,
Hail oh night and food-rich earth – yeah:
Look upon us with mild eyes – yeah
And give us all the victory.

Hail, oh Aesir, hail, oh Aesir-women,
Hail to you, oh fruit-rich soil – yeah!
Word and wisdom give us both – yeah,
And healing hands at all the times!

V 3. b) Aesir

Text: traditional, Germanic (Lancashire, England)
Melody: Harry Eilenstein

The following saying was not recorded until about 1880 AD, but it is obviously very old, since it still addresses Wotan/Odin ("Wod") and Loki ("Lok") for help. "God" is presumably the Christian god Father, but the former sungod-godfather Tyr was also sometimes called "Almighty God."

Throice I smoites with Holy Crok,
With this mell oi throice dew knock,
One for God,
An' one for Wod,
An' one for Lok.

Thrice I strike with holy crook,
With this hammer I knock thrice:
Once for God,
and once for Wotan
and once for Loki.

   In the original language these sentences rhyme, of which the second line even still contains the varied repetition of the first line, which is typical for the spell-verse "galdr-lag" of the Teutons.

   The word "mell" is the Latin "malleus" for "hammer".

   The original English text has a passing verse meter and also a passing, five-fold end rhyme, so that it is appropriate to use the original text for the spell song. Moreover, 16 of the 24 spoken vowels are an "o" or "oi" – a continuous "vowel rhyme", so to speak.

*<u>Throice</u> I <u>smoites</u> with <u>Holy</u> **<u>Crok</u>**,*
*<u>With</u> this <u>mell</u> oi <u>throice</u> dew **<u>knock</u>**,*
*<u>One</u> for **<u>God</u>**,*
*An' <u>one</u> for **<u>Wod</u>**,*
*An' <u>one</u> for **<u>Lok</u>**.*

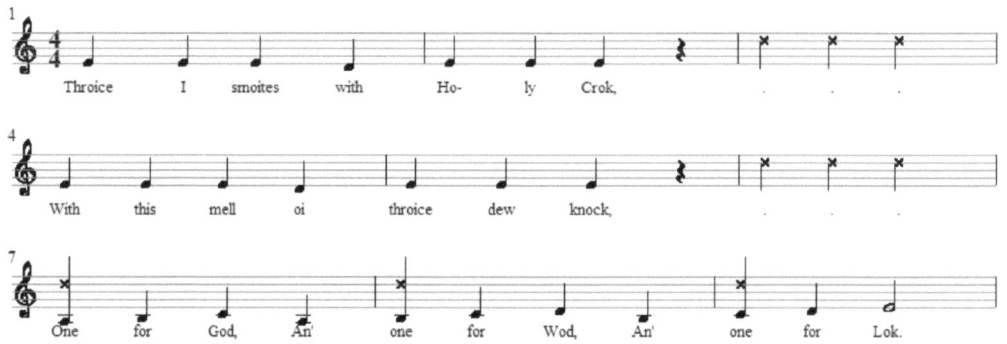

   For the notes that do not have a circle but a cross as a "head", there is a clapping in each case – in the first two lines at the end three times each and in the last line, at

41

each of the three "ones" at the beginning of the line once. This is the knocking ("knock") or hammering ("smoites") described in these invocation verses.

V 3. c) Aesir

Text and melody: Harry Eilenstein

Hönir: priest god
Tyr: the former sungod-godfather
Thor: the god of thunder
Freyr: the god of fertility, harvest and prosperity
Rig: byname of the sky guardian Heimdall
Har: epithet of the new father of the gods, Odin.

V 3. d) Sky god

Lyrics and melody: anonymous, from the Wiccan tradition.

This song has the same melody as the song "We all come from the Goddess".

The lyrics in the original are slightly different from the one given above. However, the number of syllables in the original text does not fit the melody, especially in the last line.

Original text:
We all come from God
And to him we shall return
Like a spark of fire
Soaring to the heavens.

Altered text:
We all come from the Sky-God
And to him we shall return
Like a spark of fire
Up to heaven.

V 2. e) Sun God

Text and melody: anonymous (Amerindian inspired)

V 3. f) Sun

Text and melody: Caballeros del Sol ("Knights of the Sun") (Spain)

So - leil,   So - le,   Son - ne,   Sol

The last two notes, which have an "x" instead of an "o" as "head", are clapped. The second "x" note is exactly in time, i.e. it is placed where "leil" starts in the 1st measure and "-le" in the 2nd measure, i.e. at the beginning of the 2nd quarter in the 2/4 measure. The first "x" note is a quick suggestion before the second note. During this clap, which adds a definite extra oomph to the very simple song, you breathe in again for the next singing of the four names of the sun.

The song originates from the Spanish Caballeros del Sol. These "Knights of the Sun" are a spiritual-ecological order and, so to speak, the male counterpart to the Wicca movement, which revives the old natural religions in new, feminist-magical-ecological oriented witchcraft circles. The "Knights of the Sun" have several temples in Spain and participate in most Rainbow meetings.

This song is very effective for driving away rain clouds and calling the sun.

V 3. g) Tyr

Lyrics and melody: Harry Eilenstein

A- lu Tei- . waz, An- sus Thu- ri- saz; So- wi- lo Da- gaz U- . ruz, Tei- . waz!

A- lu Tei- . waz, Rai- dho Eh- waz Al- giz Al- giz A- lu Tei- . waz!

Tyr is the former sungod and godfather of the Teutons. The text consists of the rune names, which have been named after elements from the Tyr myths, and of the invocation formula "Alu".

Alu Teiwaz,   Ansuz Thurisaz: Sowilo Dagaz Uruz, Teiwaz!
Alu Teiwaz,   Raidho Ehwaz   Algiz Alu Teiwaz!

Alu   = invocation formula
Teiwaz   = Tyr
Ansuz   = Aesir (god)
Thurisaz = thorn, sword, giant = Tyr
Sowilo   = sun = Tyr
Dagaz   = sun, brightness, day = Tyr
Uruz   = water (Tyr is in the water-underworld at night)
Raidho   = wheel (sun wheel), journey (the course of the sun (Tyr) in the sky)
Ehwaz   = horse (in front of Tyr's sun chariot)
Algiz   = two moose or deer (in front of Tyr's sun chariot)

V 3. h) Star dance

Lyrics and melody: traditional, Pawnee (Nebraska, Kansas, South Dakota).

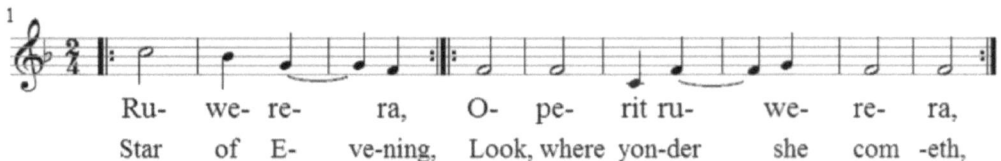

This song is sung spirited and rousing.

There are many verses to this Ghost Dance song and new ones are often invented spontaneously while singing. The stanzas are changed in the Ghost Dance each time one of the dancers pretends that he cannot continue dancing at the end of the stanza. The dance begins in the evening and ends in the morning.

Some of these stanzas (not all of which fit the invocation of the moon) are:

Ruwerera, ruwerera, Atius ruwerera, Atius ruwerera.
Father-Sun (2x), Look, where yonder he cometh (2x)

Ruwerera, ruwerera, Atira ruwerera, Atira ruwerera
Mother Moon (2x), Look, where yonder she cometh (2x)

45

Ruwerera, ruwerera, Operit ruwerera, Operit ruwerera
Star of Evening (2x), *Look, where yonder she cometh* (2x)

Ruwerera, ruwerera, Operit ruwerera, Operit ruwerera
Star of Morning (2x), *Look, where yonder she cometh* (2x)

Rerawha-a, rerawha-a, Atira rerawha-a, Atira rerawha-a
Stars of heaven (2x), *Lo, the many are coming* (2x)

Operit is the morning star and the evening star, both of which are Venus – the verse "Operit ruwerera" therefore has two translations.

V 3. i)   Shiva

Text and melody: probably traditional, India

Shiva, Shiva, Shiva Shambo
Shiva, Shiva, Shiva Shambo

Maha Deva Shambo
Maha Deva Shambo
Maha Deva Shambo
Maha Deva Shambo

Jaya, Jaya, Shiva Shambo
Jaya, Jaya, Shiva Shambo

Maha Deva Shambo
Maha Deva Shambo
Maha Deva Shambo
Maha Deva Shambo

Shiva:	god of meditation, ecstasy, dance and kundalini
Shambo:	"place of joy" (an epithet of Shiva)
Maha Deva:	"great god" (an epithet of Shiva)
Jaya:	"victory" (enlightenment)

V 3. j) Ganesha

Text and melody: probably traditional, India

The elephant god is the helper in foundations and beginnings of all kinds. He helps to remove obstacles from the way. His name means "master of his retinue."

Om:	internalization, directing the life force by means of the third eye
gam:	the mantra for meditation on Ganesha
Ganapataye:	epithet of Ganesha; also means "lord of the retinue"
namaha:	worship

47

V 3. k) Osiris

Lyrics and melody: Harry Eilenstein

Ancient Egyptian ("hieroglyphic language"):

Ausar netjer nefer
Ausar ib-i hotep
Ankh her udja reshut
Ankh her udja reshut
Heri ta her cheri pet
Heri ta her cheri pet

Osiris, good god,
Osiris, God in my heart:
Life, health and joy
Life, health and joy –
On earth and under heaven!
On earth and under heaven!

V 3. l) Pan

Text and melody: Harry Eilenstein

Pan is a Greek god with goat legs and goat horns who lives in the wilderness. He was originally the (male) ancestors in the afterlife who changed into a he-goat when they re-procreated themselves together with the otherworld Goddess – this re-procreation preceded their rebirth.

Hey Io Pan, Io Pan, Io Pan!
Hey Io Pan! Hey Io Pan!
Play your flute to our dance!
Hey Io Pan! Hey Io Pan!
Give us more than just one glance!
Hey Io Pan! Hey Io Pan!
Bring us joy with cup and lance!
Hey Io Pan! Hey Io Pan!
You are our life's great chance!
Hey Io Pan! Hey Io Pan!

Pan, Pan, Pan! Pan, Io Pan!
Pan, Pan, Pan! Pan, Io Pan!

The "x" notes in the last line are sprechgesang („rap"), shouting, and possibly clapping.

"Cup and Lance" refers to Pan's favorite activity along with the nymphs – when he's not playing his reed flute ….

You can also sing the chant with fewer verses – or add some more – or sing the song with precentor (1st half of the line) and chorus (2nd half of the line).

The tempo is approximately andante at the beginning and then gradually gets faster. If the whole thing dissolves into chaos and laughter when the tempo eventually gets too fast, it doesn't matter – that is entirely in accordance with the spirit of Pan.

V 3. m)   Ma Yin Bo sei

Lyrics and music: traditional (Japan)

As with many song texts, it is difficult to find out the origin of this mantra. For the correctness of the widespread opinion that this song originates from Japan, at least the last word "sei" speaks, which means "great" as "seii" in Japan. It is used in Japan also in the way as e.g. "magne" (magnus = great) in the title "Charlemagne". For example, "Great General" in Japanese is "seii-shogun". Sometimes "seii" is also added to a person's name as a general honorific (e.g. "Miyagi-sei"), similar to the Indian "-ji" and the "-ye" in the Navaho language.

Buddha Avalokiteshvara is the Buddha of compassion. He is probably the most popular figure of the Buddha. His Sanskrit name was originally composed of "avalokita" ("to perceive") and "svara" ("sound, tones") and therefore meant approximately "He who hears everything", by which is meant that Buddha Avalokiteshvara hears the complaints of all living beings and has therefore decided not to enter Nirvana until he has helped all living beings to go with him at the same time. Since about 700 A.D. the name is mostly interpreted as a composition of "avalokita" ("perceive") and "ish-vara" ("Lord"), i.e. Avalokiteshvara is understood as "He who looks in all directions" or as "the Lord of all that we see (i.e. the world)".

In Tibet, under the name "Chenrezig" or "Spyan-ras gzigs" ("the one with the compassionate gaze"), he is the patron saint of the country. The Dalai Lama is regarded by Tibetans as an incarnation of Buddha Avalokiteshvara.

In Mongolia, Buddha Avalokiteshvara is called "Nidubarüsheckchi", which is a literal translation from Tibetan.

Buddha Avalokiteshvara was also often identified with the Mother Goddess, which gave rise to the Buddha Mother Goddess "Kuan-Yin" ("who hears all lamentations") in China, for example. This name is composed of "Kuan" ("to consider") and "yin" ("sound"), which corresponds quite exactly to the meaning of Avalokiteshvara. In Korea this Buddha mother goddess is called "Kwan-Am", in Vietnam "Quan The Am" and in Thailand "Chao Mae Kuan". In Japan, Buddha Avalokiteshvara is also considered a goddess and is worshipped as Sho Kannon. These names are all phonetic evolutions of Kuan Yin.

"Ma Yin Bo Sei" therefore seems to be first of all a Japanese name with the honorific "Seii" at the end.

The syllable "Ma" is probably identical with the name component "Am" in the Korean name and "Mae" in the Thai name Buddha Avalokiteshvaras and would mark "Ma Yin Bo sei" thereby as a mother goddess.

"Bo" is probably a short form of Buddha and could therefore be translated as "enlightened".

The syllable "Yin" is very probably identical with the "Yin" in the name of the Chinese Buddha mother goddess "Kuan-Yin".

One could translate the name "Ma Yin Bo Sei" as "the revered ("sei") mother goddess ("Ma") of Buddhism ("Bo"), who hears all complaints ("Yin")". Another possibility would be "the revered ("sei") and enlightened ("Bo") mother goddess ("Ma") who helps all complainers ("Yin")". These two translations of the name "Ma Yin Bo Sei" correspond exactly to the character of Buddha Avalokiteshvara as mother goddess and female boddhisattva respectively in China, Korea, Japan, Vietnam and Thailand.

Thus, the name "Ma Yin Bo Sei" is not specifically Japanese, but rather generally "Far Eastern".

V 4. Animal Songs

V 4. a) Snake

Text and melody: Harry Eilenstein

The snake symbolizes the ancestors, the underworld and the afterlife path, as well as kundalini and life force in general. It also stands for looking at the small, the hidden and the moment.

Dragon, Serpent, Kundalini
Fire glowing, coming up to me;
Wake my chakras, wake my fire,
slither through my life-full body;
hey hey hey Dragon, hey hey hey Serpent
let my life be joy!

V 4. b) Bear

Text and melody: traditional, Pawnee (Kansas, Nebraska)

The bear symbolizes strength, self-reliance, and self-assertion.

The Pawnees lived on the northeastern prairies of Nebraska and Kansas and were neighbors of the Cheyenne and the Dakotas, among others.

This very old song was probably originally sung at the reception of the Bear warriors when they returned from a battle at sunrise. Later, the Bear clan of the Pawnees sang it at their sunrise ceremonies.

In Pawnee mythology, the bear receives its power from Grandfather Sun and is therefore closely associated with him. The Pawnee word for bear is "kuruks" and appears only in the title of the song, but not in its lyrics.

This song has a second stanza in which instead of the bear warriors, the sun rays are greeted – the bear warriors and the sun rays being magically linked and equated.

> *Rasakura rukuksa rerawha*
> *Rerawha rerawha rera e-yo!*
> *Rasakura rura whia rerawha rera e-yo!*

The meaning of these lines is:

> *Now the Sun has sent his rays to Earth,*
> *they are coming, they are coming, they are many, e-yo!*
> *Sunbeams o'er the ground are speeding, they are many, e-yo!*

V 4. c)   Eagle

Text and melody: traditional, Arapaho (northern prairie)

The eagle symbolizes the overview and the focus on the goals and on the big picture.

This song gets its dynamics from the fact that the sentences of the text always begin on the last quarter of the previous bar, and thus one never "finishes" the song, so to speak: when one finishes singing the bar, a new sentence has already begun, and when one finishes singing the sentence, a new bar has already begun. One flies on and on as an eagle, so to speak … The same musical structure is also found in the song "We all come from the Goddess".

In the notes above, for the sake of clarity, rests are indicated at the beginning and at the end of each movement. Between two movements, however, these are not added to a 5/4 long pause, but the pauses are always only 1/4 long – as in line 1 between "around" and "we circle" or as at the beginning of line 2 between "around" and "the boundries".

Whether this most famous of all Eagle songs actually originated with the Arapahos cannot be determined for lack of a text in the Arapaho language.

V 4. d)　Eagle

Text and melody: traditional, probably Arapaho (northern prairies)

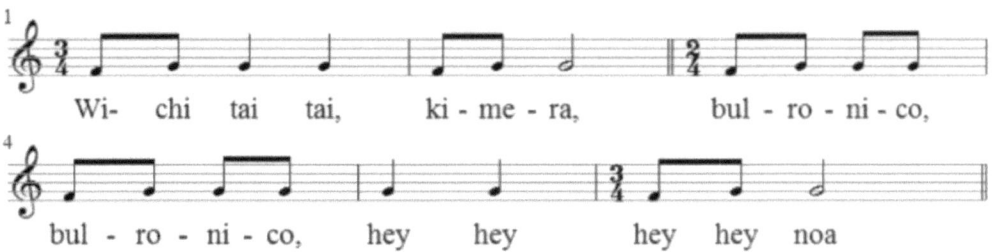

Presumably this is an Arapaho eagle song, as the words "Wichi tai" also appear in other Arapaho eagle songs. This song has also been used as movie music, with these Native American verses each followed by the phrases *"War-spirit's feet are swinging round my head; makes me feel glad that I'm not dead."*

Presumably this is a new addition and not a translation of the Arapaho text – if only because the Arapaho text is far too short for such extensive content. Moreover, the Arapaho language consists largely of much longer and more complexly constructed words (prefixes, endings, etc.) than the words in the English song text.

V 4. e) Eagle

Lyrics and melody: traditional, probably Arapaho (northern prairie).

Fly like an ea-gle, fly-ing so high,

cir-ce-ling the u-ni-vers on wings of pure light.

Hey wit-schi tai tai, wit-schi tai-o,

hey wit-schi tai tai, wit-schi tai-o.

There are many variants of this song, all of which probably trace back to a single song that may have originally come from the Arapahos.

V 4. f) White Buffalo Woman

Lyrics and melody: Harry Eilenstein

The White Buffalo Woman ("Pte-san-win") symbolizes the community.

White Bu-ffa-lo Wo-man, milk and warmth and lo-. ving arms, Pte-san-win Pte-san-win

White Buffalo Woman
Milk and warmth and loving arms
Pte-san-win, Pte-san-win

The "x" notes at the end are half sung, half spoken/shouted ("chanting").

V 4. g) Wolf

Text and melody: traditional, Dakota (North and South Dakota, Minnesota).

He ya a he ya a ah Hai ha e ya ha ah

Ha - ah he ya hu i yu yu

Hu Hu Hu

This "song of the wolf spirit" ("Sung-Manitou Olowan") was learned at night by the Dakota chief Gray Horse when he was 27 years old on the warpath, from the wolves themselves. The wolves and also the dogs, who were then still very similar to the wolves, were the symbols and allies of the warriors among the Dakota and among most of the other Plains Indians.

The same conception is found also with the Indo-Europeans, with whom the warrior alliances called themselves also wolves and dressed themselves in wolf skins. Among the Germanic tribes, for example, the Ulfhedinn warriors ("wolf skin") are found next to the Berserker bear shamans ("bear skin"). From this tradition, which can also be found among the Dacians, Thracians, Scythians, Romans, Hittites, Slavs and other Indo-European peoples, the werewolf legends arose later, because there was the idea that the warriors turned into wolves before the battle. This goes back ultimately to the fact that the warriors called the wolf spirit into themselves before the fight and filled themselves with it and thus in a certain way actually became wolves.

In the Germanic sagas it is described several times, how a warrior put himself into the wolf or bear ecstasy, in which he stomped, shouted and bit into the edge of his wooden shield.

This symbolism has been preserved until today. For example, in the 3rd Reich, submarine squadrons were called "wolf packs" and in English there is the pejorative term "dogs of war" for mercenaries.

An inverted "v" over a note means that this syllable is emphasized and sung a little louder. The last line mimics the howling of wolves.

V 4. h)   White She-Wolf

Text and melody: Harry Eilenstein

The mother goddesses of the animals are very often seen on dream journeys as an animal of the animal species in question, which, however, is about twice as large and consists of a milky white, semi-transparent mist (life force). Therefore, these animal mother goddesses are called "White Buffalo Woman", "White Wolf Woman", "White Elephant" etc. by very many peoples. Sometimes, though much more rarely, also "Great" is used instead of "White".

Moonlight, sniffing all, running fast, houling loud – Uuuuuh!
White Wolf, Mother Wolf, Great Wolf, Moon-Wolf – Uuuuuh!

V 4. i)   Hawk

Lyrics and melody: traditional, Pawnee (Nebraska, Kansas)

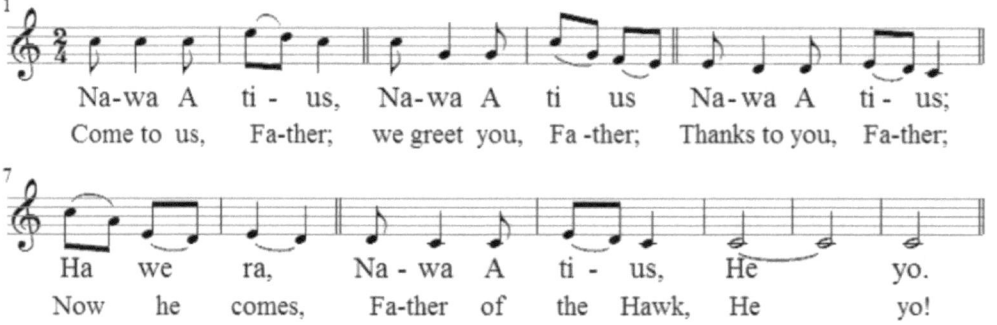

This song to the hawk father has the same melody as the Pawnee song to the corn mother.

V 5.   World Tree

V 5. a)   Heynitede

Text and melody: traditional, Native American (northern prairie).

V 5. b)   The World Tree

Lyrics and melody: Harry Eilenstein

World-Tree, highest Tree,
Leaves in heaven:
Send us light and send us life!
Roots deep down in Mother Earth.
Send us our totem!
Show us our soul!
Sky, Earth and Tree,
I rest in front of thee!

Totem = power animal, spirit animal

V 6. Elves

V 6. a) Elves

Text: J.R.R. Tolkien
Melody: Harry Eilenstein

The complete song can be found in the third chapter of the first volume of "The Lord of the Rings". It is addressed to the elf queen Elbereth. You can also use it to calm yourself, for example, if you have a diffuse fear at night in a dark forest.
The first stanza reads:

> *Snow-white! Snow-white! O Lady clear!*
> *O Queen beyond the Western Seas!*
> *O Light to us, that wander here*
> *amid the world of woven trees!*

You may also use the version in the Elven-language that was crated by Tolkien:

> *A Elbereth Gilthoniel,*
> *silivren penna míriel*
> *O menel aglar elenath!*
> *na-chaered palan-díriel*

> *Gilthoniel a Elbereth,*
> *o galadhremmin ennorath,*
> *Fanuilos, le linnathon*
> *nef aear, sí nef aearon!*

V 7.   The four elements

V 7. a)   The four elements

Lyrics and melody: Fred Hageneder (from the MC "Y Saith Gwteiddyn")
German translation: Harry Eilenstein

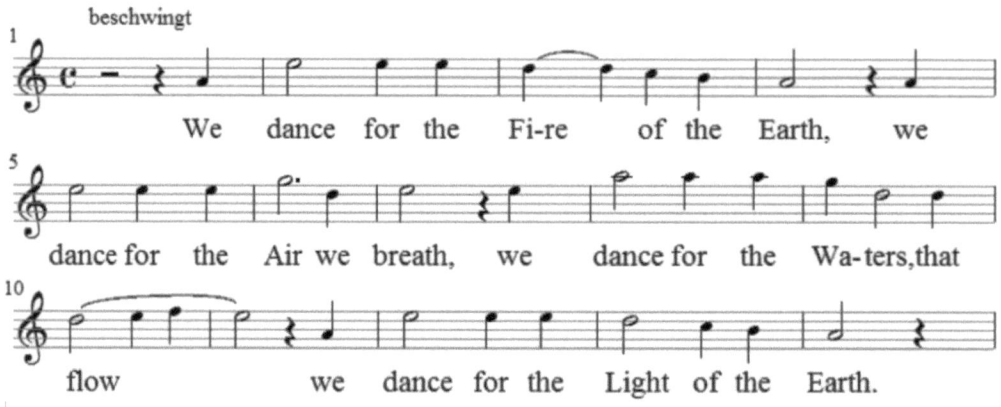

This song can also be sung in German with a slightly different melody:

Depending on the occasion when you use the song, you may also replace "dance" with "sing" respectively "tanzen" with "singen" in the lyrics.

V 7. b) The four elements

Lyrics and melody: anonymous (non-Amerindian)

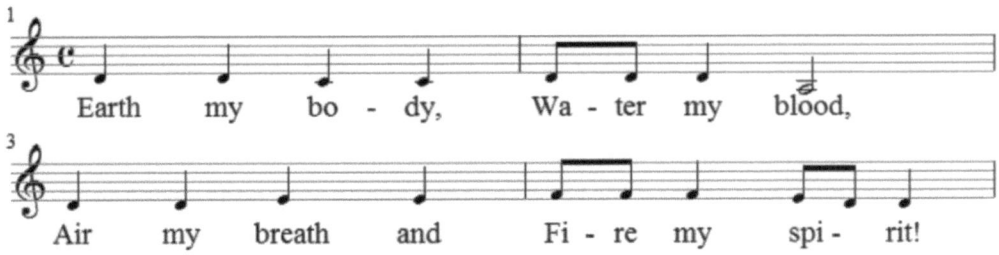

This song is very powerful and one should not use it right away as the first one in the ritual, since it already needs a foundation, so to speak, in order to build on it to create an increase. This song is clearly ecstatic and not meditative.

This effect can be increased by the main singer singing after a while a fifth higher than before. Experience shows that some of the other singers then also change to the higher pitch, while others remain at the original pitch. This creates an even higher intensity of the singing.

From the notes, this simple two-part harmony looks like this:

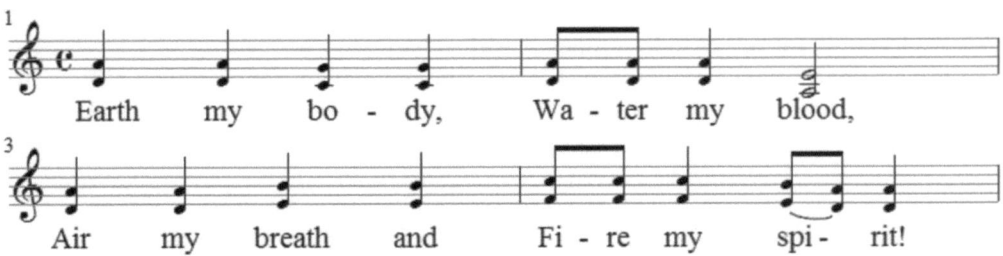

Towards the end of the song, the main singer should then return to the original pitch so that the intensity evoked can settle into the singers and come back to rest.

It makes sense not to end this song suddenly, but to gradually get quieter at the end and then stop. Afterwards, everyone should be given enough time to feel the evoked power within themselves.

V 7. c) Fire

Text and melody: anonymous, Amerindian inspired

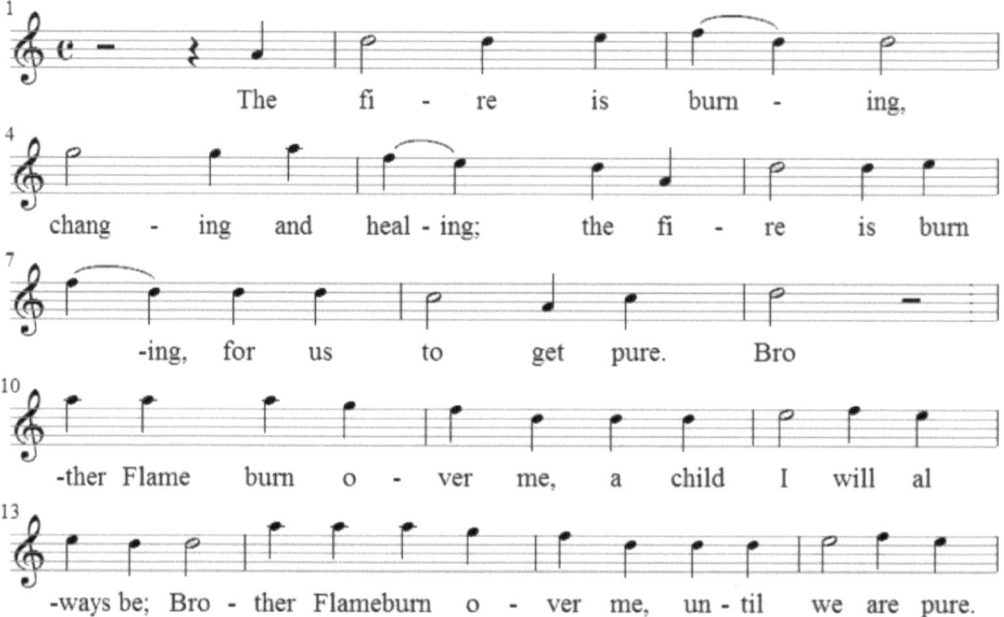

The melody of this song corresponds to that of the song "The river is flowing".

The original text of this stanza says "destroying" instead of "changing". But this word has one syllable too many and therefore does not fit into the melody. Therefore, it seems to me to make sense to replace it with "changing" or "ending".

In the original, instead of "Brother Flame", the expression "Violet Flame" is found, although one should actually expect "Brother Flame" here because of the other three stanzas, in which "Mother Earth", "Father Sun" and "Sister Moon" are found.

V 7. d) Fire

Lyrics and melody: Denean (from the CD "Fire-Prayer")

In the original, the last line is "dry these tears I've cried". The verse suggested above fits better, in my opinion, with the more incantatory character of the rest of the song's text.

V 7. e)   Water

Text and melody: Native American (probably northern prairie)

Hey   we- yo   hey,   hey   we- yo   hey,   we- yo
hey,   we- yo   hey,   we- yo   ha,   we- yo   hey.

The lyrics of this song are not translatable, since they are inspirations during a vision quest. Such lyrics are in a way like long and complex names for the experience in the vision. By these "names", the power that was obtained in the vision can then be awakened or summoned again.

V 7. f)   Wind

Text and melody: Bob Wilkerson (probably a traditional Amerindian song)

I - ni wa - tchi - ne   wa - tchi - ne   a - he   we-   lo.
A - he   we-   lo,   i - ni wa - tchi   ne   i - ni   wa - tchi - ne.

This song is from more recent times by Bob Wilkerson – maybe he just recorded it.
It was either brought back from a dream trip (in which case the words would be unusually differentiated) or it is a variation on a term from a Native American language. Also the straight 4/4 time rather speaks for a not-Amerindian composition, since most Amerindian songs have a "mixed" time, consisting of 2/4 beats and 3/4 beats. However, the melodic line is reminiscent of some other Native American songs.

V 7. g)   Wind

Text: anonymous, Germanic (Scandinavian)
Melody: Harry Eilenstein

This spell comes from the saga about King Sverri: "Thou bountiful king on the high seat of the sun, we beseech Thee, grant this army a swift breeze to Bergen!"
The "king on the high seat of the sun" is the former sungod-godfather Tyr.
With verse meter and lines of equal length, it becomes:

Gaben-froher König
auf der Sonne Hochsitz,
Sei uns wohlgesonnen:
Send uns gute Winde!

Or in English with a slightly altered melody:

Gift-bestowing king
on the high seat of the sun,
Be well-disposed to us:
Send us friendly winds!

V 8. The Community

V 8. a) Welcome

Lyrics and music: traditional, Chamush (Southern California)

This song, like "We all come from the Goddess," has an "interlaced beat," meaning that the text does not fit into the measures, but that the phrases almost always extend into the following measure. This tends to make the singers sing on and on – after all, you can only ever finish the lyrics or the measure, but never both at the same time. The 1/8 rest in the last measure always joins the 5/8 rest of the first measure – you just sing on without a rest.

V 8. b)   Family

Text and melody: probably traditional, Swahili language (East Africa) (known by the band "Black Blood" as "A.I.E. a Mwana" – you may find it on youtube)

aiea mwana ninakwenda kwetu, pamoja na bibi na batoto wote
= I am going home with my wife and all our children.

aiea mwana sasa iko usiku, tunachoka nini, tuta lala naye
= It is dark now, we are tired, we are going to sleep.

baba mama rafiki, bagi ye ni muzuri
= Father, mother, friends – all are good.

watoto yote yetu, bagi ye ni muzuri
= All our children – they are all good.

baba mama rafiki, bagi ye ni muzuri
= Father, mother, friends – they are all good.

tunapenda we, hadi sante sana
= We love you and thank you very much.

tunapenda we, hadi sante sana
= We love you and thank you very much.

As an alternate chant, the song is structured as follows:

1.   (woman) *aiea mwana*
        (chorus) *ninakwenda kwetu,*
        (chorus) *pamoja na bibi*
        (chorus) *na batoto wote*

2.   (woman) *aiea mwana*
        (chorus) *sasa iko usiku,*
        (choir) *tunachoka nini,*
        (choir) *tuta lala naye*

3.   (man) *baba mama rafiki,*
        (choir) *bagi ye ni mzuri*
        (man) *watoto yote yetu,*
        (choir) *bagi ye ni mzuri*
        (man) *baba mama rafiki,*
        (choir) *bagi ye ni mzuri*

4.   (chorus) *tunapenda we,*
        (choir) *hadi sante sana*
        (chorus) *tunapenda we,*
        (chorus) *hadi sante sana*

Allegretto

a- i- e- a mwa- na; ni- na- kwen- da kwe- tu, pa- mo- ja na bi- bi na ba- to- to wo- te.

a- i- e- a mwa- na; sa- sa i- ko u- siku, tu- na- cho- ka ni- ni, tu- ta la- la na- ye.

ba- ba ma- ma ra- fi- ki, ba- gi ye ni mu- zu- ri;

wa- to- to yo- te ye- tu, ba- gi ye ni mu- zu- ri;

ba- ba ma- ma ra- fi- ki, ba- gi ye ni mu- zu- ri;

tu- na- pen- da we, ha- di san- te sa- na; tu- na- pen- da we, ha- di san- te sa- na.

V 8. c)   Ancestors

Text and melody: traditional, Ewe (Ghana, West Africa)

Adsia dogbelo, meka we enyoto milayowoda;
Adsia dogbelo, meka we enyoto milayo.
Yokoto adiga, todemea yokoto adigo, milewoge;
Adsia dogbelo, meka we enyoto milayo.
Laleh mulo, lale ma hewa,
yeddekanetschitodome laleh mu loh.

The first four lines are sung very powerfully, while the last two lines should sound very soft and melodic. The transition at the syllable "he-" in the second to last line from e to f-sharp should be soft. The transition at the last syllable of the song ("-lo") is very smooth: first the e is held, then the note slowly descends to the d and is then held there.

The lyrics of this song mean, *"Do you hear the Yokoto drums? The ritual begins! Come, let us go. Come, ancestors from the bush, join us for the festival!"*

The Yokoto drums are the large ceremonial drums with a very deep bass. They are a about 2m high and are played with drumsticks bent in an S-shape, so that you can play the drumhead, so to speak, from below, which you can't even see as a drummer because it is so far up.

"Adigo" means "to sound"; "todemea" means "do you hear?".

This is a song of the Ewe tribe in Ghana and is taught by the Kalifi ("fire of life") drum and dance group under the direction of Papafiu (Ebenezer Quartay), among others. It is usually sung to a circle dance, which has a special basic step of alternately stamping the floor twice with the left foot and twice with the right foot.

V 8. d) Love

Lyrics and melody: probably traditional, Hopi (Arizona) (handed down by Foster Perry).

The Hopi word "shima" means "love." Whether it is a traditional song is uncertain – it was handed down by Foster Perry. The song may be sung in two voices with the upper fifth in a simple way.

V 9.   The vision quest

V 9. a)   Vision Quest

Text and melody: anonymous (Amerindian?)

If this song is Native American, then it was probably originally sung in preparation for a vision quest. However, it also fits very well before any other occasion where one takes a major step into "new territory".

The second line, which emphasizes bringing one's experiences back to one's community and then sharing them with them, suggests a Native American origin, as this idea is not particularly common in the Western world with its emphasis on individualism.

Re-lease your mind, see what you find, bring it on home to your peo - ple

V 9. b) Initiation

Text and melody: traditional, Chippewa (Canada, northern USA)

The Chippewa, also called Ojibwa or Ojibwe, belong to the large group of Indians who speak an Algonkin language. They call themselves Anishinabe, which means "First People".

The initiation may refer to the separation of children from their mothers at about 7 years of age or to the vision quest.

V 10.   Sun Dance Songs

V 10. a)   Sun Dance

Text and melody: probably Amerindian (northern prairie?)

Kuaté lenjo lenjo maoté i-ano i-ano i-ano

Since the words of this song are not to be found in the complete lexicon of Amerindian languages, the text, if it should be an Native Indian song, would have to originate from a vision quest and have been written in a not known language, i.e. in the "spirit language" (as it is often the case with such visions). As a rule, however, such "vision texts" do not sound as clearly like concrete words as the words in this song.

The origin of this widespread song seems to have been forgotten – at least there is no clear indication anywhere where it came from. There is widespread agreement that it is a sun dance song. This view is also consistent with the English text.

The English variant of this song has a slightly different melody in the second and third measures, since the English text does not have the same syllable length as the original text and the melodic line does not match the distribution of root syllables in the English words.

75

V 10. b) Sun dance

Text and melody: traditional, Arapaho (Wyoming, Colorado, Kansas, Nebraska, South Dakota).

O hai ya ha, o hai ya ya hai!

He-da- wu-na-ne- i- na, Hish-ish hi ha ni- sa- na!
O may he take pi-ty on us, Fa- ther Sun, o my fa- ther!

O hai ya ya ha, yo ha hi na, o na ha u hu!

This song is addressed to the supreme deity, Ichebeniatha. His name means "the one high up there". This god is seen as the sky or the sun and is addressed as "father" or "grandfather" to express his superior position in relation to the speaker.

The Amerindian title is "Hasse Naad". "Hasse" means "raw, untanned buffalo hide" and refers to the buffalo hide used in the ritual. "Naad" means "song."

In this song there are two typical musical features of the songs of the Arapahos, but also of other Plains Indians: On the one hand the 3/4 measures inserted into the 2/4 time and on the other hand the descending tone sequence with tone repetition in the middle, which usually consists of four eighth notes and occurs in this song, for example, in the third and in the last measure of the second line as "c sharp – h – h – a".

V 11. The Chakras

There are two chants each for the seven Chakras – fourteen chants in all. The first of each of these seven pairs of chakra chants can be sung either in one voice (only the upper note line) or in two voices (the upper and the lower note line). The melody is always the same for each of the first chakra chants.

The syllable that is constantly repeated in the song is the traditional Indian mantra of that chakra.

The deity invoked in the song has a character related to the chakra in question. One can, of course, choose another appropriate deity that one is more familiar with.

The description of light and heat ("glowing," "burning," "shining," etc.) in the first song of the seven pairs of chakra chants corresponds to the perception of the chakra in question.

The terms at the end of the first chant of these seven pairs of chants ("joy", "truth", "wealth", etc.) correspond to the qualities of the chakra in question.

Of course, one can change the texts of these chants according to one's own experiences, views, and intentions.

The second of the two chants for each chakra is shorter; the melody is different each time and adapted to the character of the respective chakra.

V 11. a) Root Chakra

Text and melody: Harry Eilenstein

V 11. b) Root Chakra

Text and melody: Harry Eilenstein

V 11. c)   Hara

Text and melody: Harry Eilenstein

Isis is the Egyptian mother-goddess.

V 11. d)   Hara

Text and melody: Harry Eilenstein

V 11. e)   Solar Plexus

Text and melody: Harry Eilenstein

Shakti ist the Indian goddess of the life force.

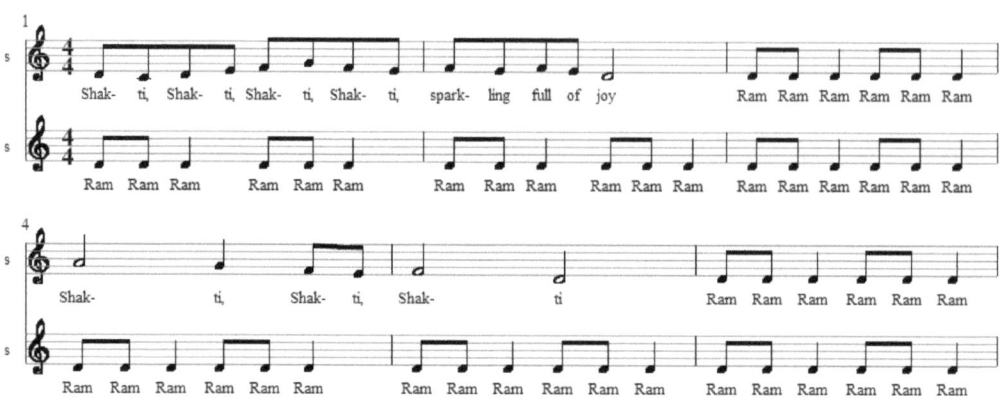

V 11. f)   Solar Plexus

Text and melody: Harry Eilenstein

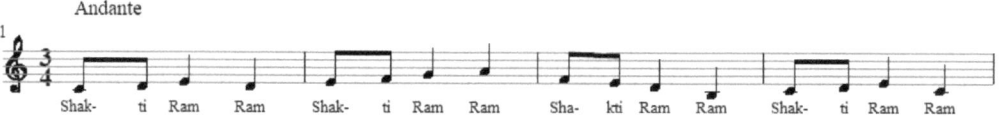

V 11. g)   Heart Chakra

Text and melody: Harry Eilenstein

"Ausar" is the ancient Egyptian spelling and pronunciation of "Osiris".

V 11. h)   Heart Chakra

Text and melody: Harry Eilenstein

V 11. i) Throat Chakra

Text and melody: Harry Eilenstein

Ma'at is the Egyptian goddess of rightness, truth, beauty and therefore of life and prosperity.

V 11. i) Throat Chakra

Text and melody: Harry Eilenstein

V 11. j)   Third Eye

Text and melody: Harry Eilenstein

Marduk is the Sumerian-Babylonian sun god and king god.
You can also sing "Om" instead of "Aum", which is probably more familiar to most.

V 11. j)   Third Eye

Text and melody: Harry Eilenstein

V 11. k)   Crown Chakra

Text and melody: Harry Eilenstein

V 11. l)   Crown Chakra

Text and melody: Harry Eilenstein

V 12.   Battle Spells and Protective Spells

This is a widespread group of spells found among almost all peoples.

V 12. a)   Battle spell

Text: traditional, Germanic (South Denmark)
Melody: Harry Eilenstein

On a gold plate amulet ("bracteate") made between 450 A.D. and 560 A.D. in the Danish village of Lellinge, there is only one magic formula, which is "salusalu". This formula can be interpreted as the S-rune ("victory" or "sun") and the formula "alu" ("holy, magic"), which was then doubled, as is often the case with magic spells not only with the Teutons. This results in the two following translation possibilities "victory magic, victory magic" or "magic of the sun, magic of the sun".

Since Tyr had been both the sungod-godfather and the war-god ("Sig-Tyr") until 500 AD, the inscription refers to Tyr in both interpretations.

Salusalu salusalu
Salusalu Tyr!

V 12. b)   Spell of liberation

Text: traditional, Germanic (Scandinavia, Iceland)
Melody: Harry Eilenstein

In the song "Gro-Galdr" ("Spell Song of Groa") the earth goddess Groa ("the green one") teaches nine spells to the young sungod Tyr-Swidag. One of them reads:

"The bands shall fall from thy limbs
and the fetters from thy feet!"

With regular verse meter and regular line length, this spell reads:

German:

> *Die Bande fallen von den Gliedern,*
> *die Fesseln springen von den Füßen!*

English:

> The bands fall from the limbs all,
> the strongest fetters leave the feet, too!

V 12. c)   Peace Treaty

Text and melody: traditional, Chippewa (Canada, northern USA)

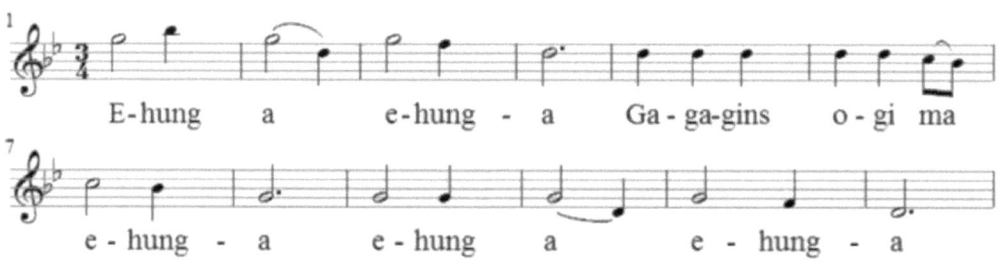

This song is sung an octave lower than the notes above indicate (If notated in the correct pitch, the combination of treble clef and bass clef would have been necessary). From the pitch, it is clear that this song was sung primarily by men.

V 12. d)   Protection Spell

Text: traditional, Germanic (Scandinavia, Iceland)
From the "Spell Song of Groa" (gro-galdr)
Melody: Harry Eilenstein

> *"The staffs of Urd shall be on all sides*
> *Be thy guards on the way that thou goest!"*

Urdar or Urd is the oldest of the norns. Her staff is her magic wand that represents the world tree. Thus this staff is a symbol of the journey up this tree to the sky, i.e. to the otherworld. Because this staff is able to protect you on the way to the otherworld it should also be able to protect you on any other way.

With regular verse and regular line length, this spell reads:

German:

> *Die Urdar-Stäbe schützen, schirmen,*
> *bewachen Dich auf allen Wegen!*

English:

> *The Urdar staffs protect and shield you,*
> *and guard you on all ways you're going!*

87

V 12. e)   Protection Spell

Text: traditional, Germanic (Scandinavia, Iceland)
From the "Spell Song of Groa" (gro-galdr)
Melody: Harry Eilenstein

"Your enemies shall be given into Your hands,
when they turn hostile against Thee!"

With regular verse meter and regular line length, this spell reads:

German:

Die Feinde fallen vor Dir nieder,
Wenn sie zu ihren Waffen greifen!

English:

The enemies fall down before Thee,
When they take up their iron weapons!

V 12. f)   Protection Spell

Text and melody: Harry Eilenstein

The four Egyptian goddesses Isis, Nephthys, Neith and Selketh guard the four corners of the sarcophagus.

"Ankh hena Sa" means "life and (magical) protection".

V 14. g)   Frigg's Travel Blessing

Text: traditional, Germanic (Scandinavia, Iceland)
From the "Wafthrudnir song"
Melody: Harry Eilenstein

Frigg: "Hail then go, hail then return, hail to thee on thy ways!"

With regular verse meter and line length, this travel blessing reads:

German:

> *Heil denn fahre immer,*
> *Heil denn kehre immer*
> *Wieder in die Heimat,*
> *Heil auf Deinen Wegen!*

English:

> *Hail then always travel,*
> *Hail return then always*
> *Back then to the homeland,*
> *Hail on all your journeys!*

The "x" notes are clapped, stomped or similar.

V 12. h)   Travel Blessing

Text: traditional, Germanic (Scandinavia, Iceland)
Melody: Harry Eilenstein

> *"May Odin be with you!"*
> > (Saga of King Olaf the Glorious).
> *"May your hands always serve you well!"*
> > (River Valley Saga)
> *"Become it as I wish it to be, and stand nothing in the way of it!"*
> > (Atli Song)

With regular verse meter and line length, this travel blessing reads:

German:

> *Mögen Deine Hände Dir gut dienen – Heil!*
> *Werde es, wie ich es wünsche – Heil!*
> *Nicht ein Hindernis auf allen Wegen!*
> *Möge Odin mit Dir sein für immer!*

English:

> *May your hands now serve you well – Hail!*
> *Be it always as I want it – Hail!*
> *Not one obstacle on every journey!*
> *Oh – may Odin be with you forever!*

Mö- gen Dei- ne Hän- de Dir gut die- . nen! Wer- de es, wie ich es wün- sche Heil!

Nicht ein Hin- der- nis auf al- len We- gen! Mö- ge O- din mit . Dir sein für im- mer!

V 12. i)   Travel Spell

Text: traditional, Germanic (Scandinavia, Iceland)
From the "Spell Song of Groa" (gro-galdr)
Melody: Harry Eilenstein

> *"To Hel they both go, Horn and Ruth,*
> *and shall the waters before Thee give way!"*

Horn and Ruth are two only very rarely mentioned rivers at the border between this world and the otherworld. In this spell they smybolize the dangers of crossing a river.

With regular verse and regular line length, this spell-song reads:

German:

> *Zu Hel führt Gjallar und auch Wimur:*
> *Die Wasser sollen von Dir weichen!*

English:

> *To Hel lead Gjallar and deep Wimur:*
> *The waters shall depart from thee here!*

Gjallar ("the loud resounding one") and Wimur ("the winding one") are two better known names of the river at the border between this world and the otherworld.

Andante

Zu Hel führt Gjal- lar und auch Wi- mur:

Die Was- ser sol- len von Dir wei- chen!

V 12. j)   Sea Voyage Spells

Text: traditional, Germanic (Scandinavia, Iceland)
From the "Spell Song of Groa" (gro-galdr)
Melody: Harry Eilenstein

> *"Never shall wind and waves harm thee*
> *and calm be the path of thy ship!"*

With regular verse meter and regular line length, this magic saying goes:

German:

> *Nie schadet Dir der Wind, die Wogen,*
> *stets friedlich sind die Meerespfade!*

English:

> *The wind, the waves shall never harm thee,*
> *and always peaceful are the sea paths!*

Andante

Nie scha- det Dir der Wind, die Wo- gen,

stets fried- lich sind die Mee- res- pfa- de!

V 12. k) Frost Protection Spell

Text: traditional, Germanic (Scandinavia, Iceland)
From the "Spell Song of Groa" (gro-galdr)
Melody: Harry Eilenstein

> *"The deadly frost shall not seize thy limbs*
> *And whole shall be thy body!"*

With regular verse meter and regular line length, this spell-saying reads:

German:

> *Der Todes-Frost soll Dich nicht fassen,*
> *Und heil soll'n Deine Glieder bleiben!*

English:

> *The deathly frost here shall not seize thee,*
> *Your limbs shall always remain healthy!*

V 12. l) Protection Spell

Text: J.R.R. Tolkien
Melody: Harry Eilenstein

This song of Tom Bombadill is found in the eighth chapter of the first volume of "The Lord of the Rings".

If you use this song, you might change "lads" for a more suitable word like "brother", "friend" and the like – you may also use a personal name. This may also go for other terms, so that it fits for your own purpose.

I have repeated the first line at the end, because it makes sense to repeat the actual intention at the end when using this song as a spell.

Wake now my merry lads! Wake and hear my calling!
Warm now be heart and limb! The cold stone is fallen;
Dark door is standing wide; dead hand is broken.
Night under Night is flown, and the Gate is open!
Wake now my merry lads! Wake and hear my calling!

94

V 13.   Special Spells

V 13. a)   Wisdom Spell

Text: traditional, Germanic (Scandinavia, Iceland)
From the "Spell Song of Groa" (gro-galdr)
Melody: Harry Eilenstein

> *"Thy heart shall have a good store of wisdom*
> *And thy mouth shall be full of wise words."*

With regular verse meter and regular line length, this spell-saying reads:

German:

> *Dein <u>Herz</u> soll <u>stets</u> voll <u>Klugheit</u> <u>leuch</u>ten!*
> *Dein <u>Mund</u> sei <u>voll</u> von <u>weisen</u> <u>Wort</u>en!*

English:

> *Thy <u>heart</u> shall <u>always</u> <u>shine</u> of <u>wis</u>dom!*
> *Your <u>mouth</u> be <u>filled</u> by <u>wi</u>sest <u>say</u>ings!*

V 13. b) Prosperity Spell

Text: traditional, Germanic (Scandinavia, Iceland)
From the Skaldskaparmal
Melody: Harry Eilenstein

> *"For this Grjotbjörn Freyr and Njörd have been richly blessed with goods and household goods."*

With regular verse and regular line length, this spell-saying reads:

German:

> *Njörd und Freyr, Wanen:*
> *segnet uns stets reichlich,*
> *Ja: mit allen Gütern!*

English:

> *Njörd and Freyr, Vanir:*
> *bless us always plenty,*
> *Yes: with many goods now!*

The Vanir (Wanen) are the one of the two tribes of the Germanic gods, to which Njörd and Freyr belong. They have been the more peaceful part of these gods. The other tribe have been the Aesir.

V 13. c)   Search for Land

Text: traditional, Celts (Ireland)
Melody: Harry Eilenstein

A song about the discovery of Ireland ("Erin") has been handed down from the druid Amairgen.

This blessing is at the same time a summons to a fertile land, for which the seafaring Celts were searching: The text starts with the seeker and leads to the land with each line beginning with the step with which the previous one ended – a word at the end of one line is repeated at the beginning of the next.

"I seek the land, the Irish isle:
Traveled be the fertile sea,
fertile the plateau,
even the rainy forest,
rain-fed the rivers with their waterfalls,
fed by waterfalls the lakes and ponds,
surrounded by ponds the hills with a spring,
a source of people the assemblies,
in the assemblies the king of Temair,
Temair, the hill of the people,
people of the sons of Mil,
the Mil barks and ships,
the high ship Erin,
Erin, high and green."

This text is much too long for a chant, and must therefore be shortened. Moreover, it should be made more general, so that it can be used as a chant in general for finding a "good place".

The principle of "steps" from the end of one line to the beginning of the next line should also be retained – one approaches one's goal step by step.

This lyrical principle can be magically supported by an imagination: One sends out one or more threads of light from one's solar plexus, which go out into the world and reach the best possible place, so that oneself is connected with this place and will then meet it. This procedure can be applied, of course, to everything that one seeks, and not only to places.

German:

> Ich _suche_ das _Land_, ich _suche_ den _Ort_,
> den _Ort_ des Gedeihens, den _Platz_ des _Friedens_,
> den _Frieden_ im _Heim_, im _fruchtbaren Feld_,
> das _Feld_ der Erfüllung hab' _ich_ nun ge_funden_.

English:

> I'm _looking_ for _land_, I'm _looking_ for _home_,
> the _place_ to _flourish_, and the _place_ of _peace_,
> the _peace_ in the _home_, in the _fertile field_,
> the _field_ of fulfillment now at _last_ I have _found_.

V 13. d) Seer Song

Text and melody: traditional, Dakota (North and South Dakota, Minnesota).

This song is sung by the shaman before the warriors go to battle, and in it he announces to each of them what their destiny will be. The circle is the circle of teepees, in the middle of which the shaman sat for a long time in a teepee built for this purpose, exploring in trance the destinies of each warrior before singing the woe and proclaiming his visions. Before singing this song, he made amulets with sacred signs for the protection of the warriors.

In this rather slow song, the catchy melody is quite striking.

Ai ya he ye, Ai ya he ye, Ai ya he ye, Ai ya he ye,

Ai ya he ye, Ai e ya e ye, Ai ya he yu he yu

Ho co - ka wan ci cu- qon yu - ton kal nun-we he ai yu
In this cir -cle, o ye war-riors, Lo, I tell you each his fu-ture

E ai yu hi e ya e ai yo he yu
All shall be as I now re -veal it; in this Cir-cle, hear you!

V 13. e) Healing Spell

Text: traditional, Germanic (Denmark)
Melody: Harry Eilenstein

Around about 800 AD, in the village of Ribe in Denmark, a human skull was described with a spell that reads as follows:

"May Ulfur and Odin and Hydyr help Buri against pain and dwarf strike!"

Ulfur ("wolf"), Odin and Hydyr are thre gods. Odin is the father of the gods, Hydyr is Hönir (priest of the gods), and Ulfur may be Tyr the god of the wolf-warriors or Loki the father of the Fenris wolf. Since Odin, Loki and Hönir often appear together as a travelling band in the German myths, Ulfur will be Loki in this context.

A "dwarf strike" is lumbago. The idea is that a dwarf has striken the ill person with a sword, a club or the like into its back. In the German language this idea is still

99

preserved in the name "Hexenschuß" ("witches shoot") of this illness.

In place of the name "Buri" one should put the name of the sick person for whom one sings this song.

According to most old spells the name of the ill person is repeated.
With regular verse and regular line length, this spell-saying reads:

German:

> *Helfe Ulfur! Helfe Odin!*
> *Helfe Hönir diesem Buri, diesem Buri!*
> *Gegen Schmerzen, gegen Leiden!*
> *Heil wird er rasch werden!*

English:

> *Help now Ulfur! Help now Odin!*
> *Help brings Hönir to this Buri, to this Buri!*
> *Pain is ousted, woe is ousted!*
> *He will soon recover!*

100

V 13. f) Healing Song

Text and melody: traditional, Cheyenne (north of the prairie)

Ta - e - va na - ma - e - yo - ni - yi,
By night I go my way un -seen

Tze - e - hu - tzit - tu na - ma - e - yo - ni - yi,
Then am I ho -ly, then have I pow'r to heal men,

Tze - e - hu - tzit - tu he yo hi yo hi yo
Then am I ho -ly, then have I pow'r to heal men,

Hai yo he yo hai yo e yo e e yo!

The Native American Nahios-si ("three fingers") belonged to the Cheyenne, who live in the north of the prairies in Colorado, Kansas, Nebraska, Wyoming and South Dakota. In her "The Indian's Book," Natalie Curtis tells the story of this song:

The power to heal was given to Nahios-si in a night vision. In a dream, he was standing upright and facing east. When day broke in his dream, a hawk appeared to him and said to him, "I have been sent to you with a message."
Then Nahios-si asked the hawk, "Who are you?" And the hawk answered, "Macha-Mahaiyu, the Great Mystery, has sent me to you to tell you that henceforth you will have the power to cure all kinds of diseases among the white people and the black people and also among your own people as well as among the animals."
Thus the hawk brought power and knowledge to Nahios-si, and the hawk also sang to him the song that Nahios-si sang henceforth when he healed.
In this way, Nahios-si became a medicine man. To heal the sick, he brewed a potion

of juniper and wild anise according to the instructions of the hawk. This potion had great healing power. Nahios-si stayed beside the sick all night and sang his healing song until just before sunrise.

And then, just as the hawk had predicted, both white people and black people, as well as people from his own people, came to Nahios-si to be healed. And for all people and animals he sang his song.

The hawk still often appeared to him in his sleep and taught him wisdom and gave him the power to heal.

This story shows a great similarity to the myths about the Grail.

The hawk, like the eagle, is the animal of the East, which is why Nahios-si is standing facing east in his dream, watching the sunrise, when the hawk appears to him.

The hawk bears great resemblance to the dove in Christianity as a symbol of the Holy Spirit.

The verse "By night I go my way unseen" could refer to astral travel, where one is also invisible to most people – but this interpretation is not certain.

The hawk could be the power animal of Nahios-si – at least power animals can help a person in life in a similar way than this hawk.

V 13. g)   Help Spell

Text: traditional, Germanic (Scandinavia, Iceland)
From the "Spell Song of Groa" (gro-galdr)
Melody: Harry Eilenstein

>*"From your shoulders shall fall, all adversity that shakes you,*
>*You shall have helpers!"*

With regular verse meter and regular line length, this spell-saying reads:

German:

Von Deinen Schultern fällt all Unbill,
Und Du sollst immer Helfer haben!

English:

All hardships fall down from your shoulders
And you shall always have good helpers!

V 13. h)   Wandering Song of the Hobbits

Text: J.R.R. Tolkien
Melody: Harry Eilenstein

This and the next song are simply feel-good songs.

Upon the hearth the fire is red,
Beneath the roof there is a bed;
But not yet weary are our feet,
Still round the corner we may meet
A sudden tree or standing stone,
That none have seen but we alone.
  Tree and flower and leaf and grass,
  Let them pass! Let them pass!
  Hill and water under sky,
  Pass them by! Pass them by!

The remaining stanzas of this wandering song of the Hobbits may be found in the third chapter of the first volume of "The Lord of the Rings".

V 13. i) Bathing Song of the Hobbits

Text: J.R.R: Tolkien
Melody: Harry Eilenstein

Sing hey! for the bath at close of day
That washes the weary mud away!
A loon is he that will not sing:
O! Water Hot is a noble thing!

The remaining stanzas of this wandering song of the Hobbits can be found in the fifth chapter of the first volume of "The Lord of the Rings".

Allegretto

Sing hey! for the bath at close of day That wa- shes the wea- ry mud a-

way! A loon is he that will not sing: O! Wa- ter Hot is a no- ble thing!

English Books by Harry Eilenstein

- Living Magic (261 p.)
- The Synthesis of Physics and Magic (192 p.)
- Telepathy for Beginners (60 p.)
- Telepathy for Advanced Learners (52 p.)
- Telekinesis for Beginners (56 p.)
- Life Force for Beginners (76 p.)
- Astral Projection for Beginners (60 p.)
- Meditation for Beginners (60 p.)
- Prophecy for Beginners (60 p.)
- Ritual Magic for Beginners (64 p.)
- Magic Chant for Beginners (108 p.)
- Invocations for Beginners (52 p.)
- Evocations for Beginners (62 p.)
- Auto-Movement for Beginners (60 p.)
- Elves for Beginners (56 p.)
- Hypnosis for Beginners (56 p.)
- Love Magic for Beginners (52 p.)
- Money Magic for Beginners (60 p.)
- Magic Objects for Beginners (64 p.)

- Shamanism for Beginners (52 p.)
- Self Knowledge for Beginners (60 p.)
- Number Symbolism for Beginners (64 p.)
- Mandalas for Beginners (76 p.)
- Crop Circles for Beginners (344 p.)
- Feng Shui for Beginners (96 p.)

These books will be puplished soon:

- Kundalini for Beginners
- Chakra-Magic for Beginners
- Astrology for Beginners
- Magic Research for Beginners
- Symbolism of Numbers for Beginners
- Language of the Moon – for Beginners
- Da'ath-Magic for Beginners
- Magic for Beginners – Anthology I
- Magic for Beginners – Anthology II
- Magic for Beginners – Anthology III
- Magic for Beginners – Anthology IV

Bücher von Harry Eilenstein

Religion allgemein
- Die sieben Schritte des Lebens (428 S.)
- Muttergöttin und Schamanen (168 S.)
- Göbekli Tepe (472 S.)
- Die Göttin von Göbekli Tepe (144 S.)
- Totempfähle (440 S.)
- Christus (60 S.)
- Dakini (80 S.)
- Vajra (76 S.)

Ägypten
- Hathor und Re 1: Götter und Mythen im
  Alten Ägypten (432 S.)
- Hathor und Re 2: Die altägyptische Religion –
  Ursprünge, Kult und Magie (396 S.)
- Isis (508 S.)

Indogermanen
- Die Entwicklung der indogermanischen
  Religionen (700 S.)
- Wurzeln und Zweige der indogermanischen
  Religion (224 S.)

Germanen
- Die Götter der Germanen (87 Bände – siehe
  nächste Seite)
- Odin (300 S.)

Kelten
- Cernunnos (690 S.)
- Taliesin (228 S.)
- Der Kessel von Gundestrup (220 S.)
- Der Chiemsee-Kessel (76)

Psychologie
- Über die Freude (100 S.)
- Das Geheimnis des inneren Friedens (252 S.)
- Das Beziehungsmandala (52 S.)
- Gefühle und ihre Verwandlungen (404 S.)
- einsgerichtet (140 S.)
- Liebe und Eigenständigkeit (216 S.)
- Von innerer Fülle zu äußerem Gedeihen (52 S.)

Heilung
- Die Symbolik der Krankheiten (76 S.)

Kunst
- Herz des Tanzes – Tanz des Herzens (160 S.)

Drama
- König Athelstan (104 S.)

Bücher von Harry Eilenstein

„Magie für Anfänger"

- Telepathie für Anfänger (60 S.)
- Telepathie für Fortgeschrittene (52 S.)
- Telekinese für Anfänger (52 S.)
- Lebenskraft für Anfänger (60 S.)
- Meditation für Anfänger (56 S.)
- Kundalini für Anfänger (100 S.)
- Hypnose für Anfänger (56 S.)
- Auto-Movement für Anfänger (56 S.)
- Chakra-Magie für Anfänger (148 S.)
- Astralreisen für Anfänger (56 S.)
- Astrologie für Anfänger (120 S.)
- Ritual-Magie für Anfänger (56 S.)
- Mandalas für Anfänger (68 S.)
- Geldzauber für Anfänger (56 S.)
- Liebeszauber für Anfänger (52 S.)
- Invokationen für Anfänger (52 S.)
- Evokationen für Anfänger (60 S.)
- Elfen für Anfänger (56 S.)
- Magie-Forschung für Anfänger (140 S.)
- Selbsterkenntnis für Anfänger (52 S.)
- Zahlensymbolik für Anfänger (60 S.)
- Die Sprache des Mondes – für Anfänger (116 S.)
- Zaubergesänge für Anfänger (100 S.)
- Zukunftschau für Anfänger (60 S.)
- Schamanismus für Anfänger (52 S.)
- Magische Gegenstände für Anfänger (68 S.)
- Da'ath-Magie für Anfänger (64 S.)
- Kornkreise für Anfänger (348 S.)
- Feng Shui für Anfänger (96 S.)
- Magie für Anfänger – Sammelband I (696 S.)
- Magie für Anfänger – Sammelband II (664 S.)
- Magie für Anfänger – Sammelband III (580 S.)

„Traumreisen"

- Traumreisen zu Heilpflanzen (700 S.)

Magie

- Handbuch für Zauberlehrlinge (408 S.)
- Tarot (104 S.)
- Physik und Magie (184 S.)
- Die Synthese von Physik und Magie (200S.)
- Die Magie-Formel (156 S.)
- Krafttiere – Tiergöttinnen – Tiertänze (112 S.)
- Schwitzhütten (524 S.)
- Mythen und Magie der Harfe (116 S.)
- Magie heute – Berichte aus der Praxis (288 S.)

Meditation

- Der Lebenskraftkörper (230 S.)
- Die Chakren (100 S.)
- Das Chakren-System mit den Nebenchakren (296 S.)
- Organe und Chakren (64 S.)
- Die platonischen Körper in den Chakren (156 S.)
- Meditation (140 S.)
- Drachenfeuer (124 S.)
- Kundalini I (676 S.)
- Reinkarnation (156 S.)
- einsgerichtet (140 S.)

Astrologie

- Astrologie (496 S.)
- Photo-Astrologie (428 S.)
- Die astrologischen Aspekte (88 S.)
- Horoskop und Seele (120 S.)

Kabbala

- Kursus der praktischen Kabbala (150 S.)
- Eltern der Erde (450 S.)
- Blüten des Lebensbaumes:
  - Die Struktur des kabbalistischen Lebensbaumes (370 S.)
  - Der kabbalistische Lebensbaum als Forschungshilfsmittel (580 S.)
  - Der kabbalistische Lebensbaum als spirituelle Landkarte (520 S.)

Die Themen der 87 Bände der Reihe „Die Götter der Germanen"